POVERTY

Raniero Cantalamessa

POVERTY

Translated by Charles Sérignat, OFM Cap.

ALBA · HOUSE alba house NEW · YORK
SOCIETY OF ST. PAUL, 2187 VICTORY BLVD., STATEN ISLAND, NEW YORK 10314

ST PAULS

Library of Congress Cataloging-in-Publication Data

Cantalamessa, Raniero.
[Povertà. English]
Poverty / Raniero Cantalamessa; translated by Charles Sérignat.
p. cm.
Includes bibliographical references.
ISBN 0-8189-0788-6
1. Poverty — Religious aspects — Christianity. I. Title.
BV4647.P6C3613 1997
248.4'7 — dc21 97-2512
CIP

Produced and designed in the United States of America by the Fathers and Brothers of the Society of St. Paul, 2187 Victory Boulevard, Staten Island, New York 10314, as part of their communications apostolate.

ISBN: 0-8189-0788-6

Printing Information:

Current Printing - first digit 1 2 3 4 5 6 7 8 9 10

Year of Current Printing - first year shown

1997 1998 1999 2000 2001 2002 2003 2004 2005

Table of Contents

Preface ix

I. "Happy are those who consider the poor"

Material Poverty: a social phenomenon to be combated 1

1. The poor exist! 1

2. "You did it to me!" 6

3. The poor to be loved, assisted and evangelized 13

II. "He became poor for your sake"

Material Poverty: an evangelical proposition to be embraced 23

1. Being "for the poor" and being "poor" 23

2. Renewal of poverty "in the Spirit" 29

3. Poverty in the life of Christ 36

4. "Blessed are you poor!" 41

5. "We have found the truly poor man!" 48

6. "We have left everything and followed you" 51

III. "You cannot serve God and wealth"

Spiritual Poverty: an evil to be combated 59

1. "You are poor!" 61

2. The idolatry of money, root of all evil 67

3. "Apart from you I want nothing on earth" 77
4. "Weep, you rich!" 81

IV. "Blessed are the poor in spirit, for theirs is the Kingdom of Heaven"

Spiritual Poverty: an ideal to strive for 89
1. The "poor" and the "poor in spirit" 92
2. The biblical ideal of poverty in spirit 100
3. How to live the beatitude of the poor 104
4. Poverty and the return to unity 111
5. "Go back inside yourself!" 119

Footnotes 125

Preface

Following the publication of the two books on *Obedience* (Boston: St. Paul Books and Media, 1989) and *Virginity* (New York: Alba House, 1995), many people asked me to give some thought to a similar study of *Poverty*, even showing surprise that it had taken so long. Let me explain the reason for the delay by letting you into a secret. Two or three times in the past I did try to deal with the subject of poverty in my Advent sermons to the Papal Household. On one occasion I had even printed and distributed the programme. But at the last minute I was always compelled to withdraw. I felt absolutely unable and unworthy to tackle the subject, lacking in respect for the poor, even hypocritical. I said to myself: how dare we talk about poverty, when what we today would consider a heroic form of poverty for ourselves is a normal fact of everyday life, if not actually a luxury, for millions of human beings? For us, fasting for life on bread and water would be the height of austerity, whereas millions of people can only dream of having "their food supplied, their water assured" (cf. Is 33:16).

How did I manage to overcome my difficulty

this time? First of all, by remembering Christ's example. In Jesus' day, in Galilee and elsewhere, there was as much mass poverty as there is today, but this did not stop Jesus from putting forward poverty as an ideal. In fact, social poverty should become one more incentive to rediscover the ideal of voluntary poverty and a simple, moderate lifestyle. After all, what is it that actually makes poor people poor and keeps them so, if not the inordinate search for riches and comfort by a few? And who but those who have chosen to be poor can really understand the poor and espouse their cause?

There is, I told myself, one person who has every right to talk about poverty today, and that is Jesus Christ. So I will let Him speak, as directly as possible. God's word is "living and enduring" (1 P 1:23). Even today it still has something new to say about poverty. So, we are going to project God's words onto our situation like beams of light, twisting them like flaming swords, or beacons scanning vast stretches of the sea at night, one after another. Or rather, they are like a mirror, and we must stand before it and see ourselves reflected in the word.

I have also found it helpful to recall the example of my Seraphic Father St. Francis. After presenting his followers with the ideal of highest poverty, he writes in his Rule: "I warn all the brothers and exhort them not to despise or judge those whom they see wearing soft and fine clothing, and enjoying luxuries in food and drink; each one should rather judge and despise himself."[1] So it is possible to talk about poverty entirely positively, without having to judge anyone except oneself. Christian preaching on poverty has always been blighted and made suspect by the tendency to demand poverty of others and use it as a charge against them.

The greatness and originality of Francis was that he broke that tendency. In an age when many cried out against the wealth and corruption of the institutional Church, he banished all criticism of others from his own life, ruled out every adversarial stance. He took no controversial stand against the hierarchical Church, nor did he argue against the heretics who did. He was the clearest example of what Yves Congar defined as "true reform of the Church — not by way of criticism, but by way of holiness."[2]

It ought to be much easier for me than it was for Francis to refrain from criticizing others. He was poor; I, unfortunately, am not, or at least not poor enough. An ancient Church Father had this advice for someone whose duty obliged him to speak about spiritual things he himself had not yet experienced in his own life: "Speak of them as a disciple, and not with authority, having humbled your soul and made yourself smaller than any of your hearers."[3] In these meditations I too will try to talk about poverty in the same way. I make my own the words of Gregory the Great when he found himself in a similar situation to mine: "I shall speak in such a way that the sword of

God's word can pass through me and pierce the heart of my neighbor. I shall speak in such a way as to be a mouthpiece for God's word, even when it is aimed against myself."[4]

Together we will stand in front of the mirror of God's word, and there "everyone is to examine himself" (1 Cor 11:28). Examine himself, not someone else. We shall try not to spend the whole time considering biblical doctrine about poverty — its development, its various forms and non-biblical parallels — without ever looking at ourselves. That, as someone once said, would be like observing the mirror and not one's own reflection in the mirror. It would be a trick to neutralize the word of God, to postpone its implementation indefinitely.[5]

The difficulty I have tried to describe so far is the *subjective* one, met with by anyone who has to talk about poverty today. But there is also an *objective* difficulty, stemming from the subject itself. Poverty is an ambiguous word. It is one of those words that can be either negative or positive: for example, the Latin word *sacer*, which can mean either *sacred* or *abominable*. Scripture itself uses the word "poverty" sometimes in a negative sense, as an evil, and sometimes positively, as a good. The same is true of the word "wealth" or "riches." The meaning of the words changes according to the changing points of view.

This ambiguity has remained, and in fact increased in the course of the centuries, so that it is now almost impossible to make any statement about poverty or riches which, under any sort of careful scrutiny, would not immediately turn out to be partially, if not completely, false. The truth is that poverty and wealth are not clear and distinct ideas. They resist all attempts at rigid rationalization.

One distinction I have read in a modern author's work has helped me overcome this objective difficulty. He distinguishes two types of poverty: one material and one spiritual, and, within each of these, two further types of poverty: one bad and one good.[6] This gives us four types of poverty which we can outline as follows:

1. *Negative material poverty*, which is dehumanizing and must be combated: poverty as a social condition that is endured;
2. *Positive material poverty*, which liberates and raises people: poverty as an evangelical ideal to be cultivated;
3. *Negative spiritual poverty*, which is the absence of spiritual wealth and of truly human values: the poverty of the rich;
4. *Positive spiritual poverty*, composed of humility and trust in God, the finest blossom on the tree of biblical poverty: the wealth of the poor.

In four chapters — corresponding to the four meditations conducted for the Papal Household in Advent 1994 — we shall deal with each of these different forms or aspects of poverty, keeping to the original Christmas setting, which is so useful for an understanding of the essential message of Christian poverty.

May the Holy Spirit, invoked in the liturgy as "Father of the poor" (*Pater pauperum*), help us to receive joyfully the good news addressed to the poor, by creating in us a "steadfast spirit" determined to put it into practice.

Biblical Abbreviations

OLD TESTAMENT

Genesis	Gn	Nehemiah	Ne	Baruch	Ba
Exodus	Ex	Tobit	Tb	Ezekiel	Ezk
Leviticus	Lv	Judith	Jdt	Daniel	Dn
Numbers	Nb	Esther	Est	Hosea	Ho
Deuteronomy	Dt	1 Maccabees	1 M	Joel	Jl
Joshua	Jos	2 Maccabees	2 M	Amos	Am
Judges	Jg	Job	Jb	Obadiah	Ob
Ruth	Rt	Psalms	Ps	Jonah	Jon
1 Samuel	1 S	Proverbs	Pr	Micah	Mi
2 Samuel	2 S	Ecclesiastes	Ec	Nahum	Na
1 Kings	1 K	Song of Songs	Sg	Habakkuk	Hab
2 Kings	2 K	Wisdom	Ws	Zephaniah	Zp
1 Chronicles	1 Ch	Sirach	Si	Haggai	Hg
2 Chronicles	2 Ch	Isaiah	Is	Malachi	Ml
Ezra	Ezr	Jeremiah	Jr	Zechariah	Zc
		Lamentations	Lm		

NEW TESTAMENT

Matthew	Mt	Ephesians	Eph	Hebrews	Heb
Mark	Mk	Philippians	Ph	James	Jm
Luke	Lk	Colossians	Col	1 Peter	1 P
John	Jn	1 Thessalonians	1 Th	2 Peter	2 P
Acts	Ac	2 Thessalonians	2 Th	1 John	1 Jn
Romans	Rm	1 Timothy	1 Tm	2 John	2 Jn
1 Corinthians	1 Cor	2 Timothy	2 Tm	3 John	3 Jn
2 Corinthians	2 Cor	Titus	Tt	Jude	Jude
Galatians	Gal	Philemon	Phm	Revelation	Rv

I

"Happy are those who consider the poor"

Material Poverty: A SOCIAL PHENOMENON TO BE COMBATED

1. The poor exist!

This first meditation is about negative material poverty, not willed by God but the fruit of sin or circumstances, not chosen but undergone, a social fact that dehumanizes those who suffer it and dishonors the society that causes or tolerates it. In a word, it is about the poor, in the most usual sense of the word.

If that is our subject, what words has God spoken that we can use as a beacon or a mirror? There are two main sayings. First, the opening words of Psalm 41: "Happy are those who consider the poor and the weak." Secondly, the well-known words of Jesus: "You did it to me... You did not do it to me" (Mt 25:40, 45).

I want to tell you at once how the following reflections came about, because this more than anything else will help us grasp the heart of the message. I had just finished writing the *Ascent of Mount Sinai* where, by using all the means provided by Scripture, Tradition and culture, I tried to arouse in people today the sense that God exists, that He is alive, that He is a reality and not an abstraction. In short, I tried to persuade them to "notice" God. All of a sudden, all the words and arguments I had used seemed to turn against me and transfer themselves to a different object: the poor. It was as if someone were shouting at me in my own words: the poor also exist! We have to "notice" them too.

The divine name, "I am there," now became the name of the poor: "We are there." We are a reality, not an abstraction. The prayer of St. Augustine, with which I ended the book: "Late have I loved You, Beauty ever ancient and ever new...," now sprang to my lips in slightly different words: "Late have I loved you, poverty ever ancient and ever new. You were with me, you surrounded me on every side, but I was not with you, I did not see you, or else I saw you only with my eyes and not with my heart. You called out to me, and your call pierced through my deafness." It was truly something breathtaking, as the philosopher said when "one day, without warning, the existence of things was suddenly revealed" to him.[1]

Perhaps the greatest sin committed against the poor is indifference, pretending not to see, "passing by on the other side" (cf. Lk 10:31). What Jesus condemned in the rich man who feasted, even more than his unbridled luxury, was his hardheartedness and insensitivity, his indifference to the poor man Lazarus lying at his gate.

We tend to set up a kind of double glazing between ourselves and the poor. The effect of double glazing, so much in use today, is to keep out cold and noise. It dilutes everything, deadens and muffles every sound. So it is with the poor: we can see them on our TV screens or in the pages of newspapers or missionary magazines, moving, bustling about, crying out, but their cries are a distant echo that never reaches our hearts. We protect ourselves from them. Scripture says of this: "You have seen many things but not observed them; your ears are open but you do not hear" (cf. Is 42:20).

In rich countries, the words "the poor!" provoke the same agitation and panic as the cry "Barbarians!" aroused in the inhabitants of ancient Rome. They anxiously built walls and sent armies to watch their borders. We do the same thing, in different ways, but history tells us it's all pointless.

The first thing to do, then, in relation to the poor is to break through the double glazing, overcome our indifference and insensitivity. We need to let our defences down, be overwhelmed by a healthy anxiety in face of the fearful misery there is in the world. The poor must get under our skin, we must, as I said, "notice" the poor. To notice means our eyes are suddenly opened, our conscience wakes up with a start, and we begin to see something that was there before, only we didn't see it. Paul VI wrote in *Evangelica testificatio*: "The persistence of poverty-stricken masses and individuals constitutes a pressing call for a conversion of minds and attitudes." The cry of the poor obliges us to "awaken consciences to the drama of misery and to the demands of social justice made by the Gospel and the Church."[2]

But the word of God itself, even before the magisterium of the Church, calls for this conversion of minds and attitudes: "Happy are those who consider the poor and the weak" (Ps 41:1): happy are those who give themselves no peace because of the poor. The reason for the terrible rebuke we read in Isaiah, against shepherds who are "blind sentinels, and dogs that cannot bark," is that " the righteous perish and no one takes it to heart (*nemo percipit corde*), the devout are taken away and no one understands" (cf. Is 56:10-57:1). The expression *percipere corde*, "to perceive with the heart," is a very good description of the inner attitude towards poverty and the poor that we need to acquire. The question is to let them into our hearts, so that they stop being someone else's problem rather than ours, and become a kind of family problem.

Imagine that one day you are watching pictures of some disaster on television — a rail crash, a road accident, a fire or a collapsed building — and you suddenly recognize a close relative among the victims: your mother, your brother or your husband. How loudly you would cry out! What a change in your heart compared to a moment ago! How interested you would become in the event! What has happened? A very simple thing: what you only noticed with your eyes and brain before, you now perceive with your heart. Well, this is what ought to happen, at least to some degree, when certain scenes of harrowing misery pass before our eyes. Are these people our brothers and sisters or not? Don't we all belong to the same human family, and is it not written that we are all "members of one another" (Rm 12:5)?

Unfortunately we can get used to anything in time, and we have grown accustomed to other people's misery. It only affects us to a degree, we almost take it for granted as inevitable. However, let us look at it from God's point of view for a moment, and try to see things as He sees them. Think of a father with seven children; at every meal the same thing happens: two of the children grab everything on the table, leaving the other five unfed. Can a father remain unmoved at such a thing? Someone once compared the earth to a spaceship in which one of the three cosmonauts on board consumes 85% of the available resources, while plotting how to take over the remaining 15% as well.

2. "You did it to me!"

Now it is time for us to stand in front of the second mirror provided by Christ's words: "You did it to me," "You neglected to do it to me!" These words have given the question of the poor a new dimension in history, making it a Christological question too. Jesus of Nazareth has identified Himself with the poor. If, as certain Church Fathers used to say, the Word assumed each human being by the very *fact* of the Incarnation, then, by the *manner* of the Incarnation He has in an altogether special way assumed those who are poor, humble and suffering, to the point of identifying Himself with them.

He who pronounced the words, "This is my body," over the bread has also spoken the same words about the poor. He spoke them when, talking about what people had done or failed to do for the hungry, the thirsty, prisoners, the naked and the stranger, He solemnly declared: "You did it to me" and "You neglected to do it to me." This is the equivalent of saying: "You remember that ragged person who needed a piece of bread, that poor person holding out his hand—it was me, it was me!"

Christ is not present in the poor person in the same way as He is in the Eucharist and the other sacraments, but He is "really," truly present in them too. He "instituted" this sign, just as He instituted the Eucharist. We could say that in the poor there is a passive presence of Christ, not an active one.

Indeed, unlike the eucharistic species and the other sacraments in general, the poor man does not necessarily always carry Christ in himself and communicate Him to those who welcome Him. The poor person is not an "effective sign" of grace, producing grace by himself, *ex opere operato*, as theologians say. So much so that a person could give away all his possessions to the poor and gain nothing from it, if he lacked love (cf. 1 Cor 13:3).

Yet we do not fully welcome Christ if we are not ready to welcome the poor person with whom He has identified Himself. Anyone who comes up to receive Christ in communion, full of fervor but with his heart closed towards the poor, is like someone who sees a friend coming towards him in the distance whom he has not seen for a long time. He is filled with joy and runs to meet him, and stands on tiptoe to kiss him on the forehead. But while doing this he does not realize that his hobnailed boots are treading on his friend's feet. The poor are the bare feet of Christ with which He still walks this earth.

I remember the first time this truth "exploded" within me in all its clarity. I was visiting a third-world country, and with each new scene of misery I saw — a child in a tattered dress, her belly swollen and her face covered in flies; a group of people running after a refuse cart, hoping to pick up something dumped in the garbage heap; a body covered in sores — I heard a voice booming inside me: "This is my body. This is my body." It literally took my breath away.

By sheer coincidence, after I had been home a few days I received a letter from someone unknown to me who had been put in touch with me. She was asking for spiritual discernment about an experience she had had. She wrote: "With the eyes of my soul I had a vision of Christ crowned with thorns and the blood running down His face. It was so real and I felt such pain that I cried many tears. Then I saw a horrible sight: a huge crowd of black children, sick and dying in the hot sun with flies all over them. It made me shudder. At the same time I was stuck to my chair, unable to get up. Then a voice said to me: 'I am there. You see those children dying of starvation? Each one is Jesus, dying!' Ever since that day"—the letter continued—"I haven't stopped collecting money for the starving. I beg alms all over the place and send the money to an orphanage in Uganda. Many people help me in this, we vie with each other." The discernment was as good as done. By their fruits you shall know them, as Jesus said.

The poor person, too, is a "*vicarius Christi*," someone who stands in Christ's place. Once again, he or she is a vicar in the passive sense, not active. Not in the sense that whatever a poor person does, it is as if it were done by Christ, but in the sense that whatever is done to the poor, it is as if it were done to Christ: "You did it to me!"

One saint who took very seriously the relationship between the presence of Jesus in the Eucharist and His presence in the poor was St. John

Chrysostom. He writes — in a well known passage inserted by the Church into the Liturgy of the Hours — "Would you honor the body of Christ? Do not despise Him in His nakedness, that is, in the unclothed poor; do not honor Him here in church clothed in silk vestments, and then pass Him by unclothed and frozen outside... What is the use of loading Christ's table with gold cups while He Himself is starving? Feed the hungry, and then if you have any money left over spend it on the altar table. Will you make a cup of gold and withhold a cup of water? What use is it to adorn the altar with cloth of gold hangings and deny Christ a coat for His back?... Adorn your house if you will, but do not forget your brother in distress. He is a temple of infinitely greater value."[3] This is a bishop talking, so it's as if he had said: "Stop bringing offerings to me, bring them to the poor"; or at least: "Bring them to the poor first, and then any leftovers to me."

The philosopher Pascal expressed the same certainty of Christ's presence in the poor, but in a different way. During his last illness, unable to receive the Viaticum because he was unable to keep anything down, he asked for a poor man to be brought into his room, so that "since I am unable to communicate in the Head, I may at least communicate in His body."[4]

Indeed, throughout the centuries Christ Himself has taken pains to confirm this strict and realistic interpretation of His words "you did it to me."

Christian hagiography abounds in episodes of a poor person receiving a kindness and later turning out to have been Jesus in person. Perhaps the most famous of these is St. Martin of Tours. One day, Martin, while still a soldier and a catechumen, met a poor man in northern Europe where he was serving, who was naked and half frozen by the cold. Having nothing with him except the cloak he was wearing, he cut it in two with a stroke of his sword, and gave one half to the poor man. That night Christ appeared to him, clothed in part of his cloak and saying with evident pride to the surrounding angels: "Martin, still a catechumen, has covered me with this cloak."[5]

The poor person is Jesus, still roaming the world unrecognized, rather like when He appeared in different guises after the resurrection to Mary as a gardener, to the disciples on the road to Emmaus as a traveller, to the apostles on the lake as an expert fisherman standing on the shore — waiting for *their eyes to be opened* with a cry of recognition: "It is the Lord!" (Jn 21:7). If only that same cry of recognition — "It is the Lord!" — could issue from our lips even once, at the sight of a poor person.

St. Leo the Great said that since the Ascension "the visible presence of our Redeemer has passed over into the sacraments of the Church."[6] We need to extend that important principle. It is true that from the sacramental point of view everything that was visible about Christ has now passed into the rites and ministries of the Church, but it is also true that existentially this visible aspect has passed to the poor and to all those He was referring to when He said: "You did it to me." A lay observer at the Council wrote: "The Council Fathers rediscovered the sacrament of poverty, the presence of Christ under the species of those who are suffering."[7]

A few years ago a man died who had enjoyed a recognized prophetic charism. During his prayer times he would often receive words from the Lord which he faithfully noted down. After his death his wife collected and published them. In one of them Jesus says: "I can only come down from the cross if you remove the nails you have hammered in. The nails are the injustices you have inflicted on the poor... I am nailed to the cross in my poor."[8]

It is now time for us to draw the consequences of all this for our understanding of the Church. At the time of the Council, John XXIII coined the expression "the Church of the poor."[9] The phrase has a far wider meaning than appears at first sight. As well as the poor people who belong to the Church, the Church of the poor embraces, in a certain sense, all the poor in the world, whether they are baptized or not. Their poverty and sufferings are their baptism of blood. If Christians are those who have been "baptized into Christ's death" (Rm 6:3), who has been baptized into Christ's death more than they?

But — you may say — the poor do not always have faith! That is true, but then do children have faith when they are brought for baptism? In that case — you insist — their parents or godparents or the Church have faith on their behalf. And I would reply, what prevents the Church from having faith on their behalf, even in this case too? Couldn't "the Church supply," as theologians say? In the case of children we say that grace prevails even over faith; God's free and gracious initiative prevails over their conscious response. Besides, did the Holy Innocents have faith? Yet we venerate them as saints. They suffered for Christ, but in the case of the poor that is not all: Christ suffers in them.

But not all the poor are good, devout or innocent! That's very true. But, just as there are good and bad Christians, tares and wheat, in the visible Church even after baptism, so there are good and bad among the poor, but all of them are still Christ's flock. How could we fail to consider them as Christ's Church in some way, when Christ Himself declared them to be His body? They are "Christians" not because they call themselves Christ's followers but because He declared that they are His, when He said "You did it to me!" If there is one case where the controversial expression "anonymous Christians" can be correctly applied, it would certainly be this one concerning the poor.

The Church of Christ is therefore much larger than current figures show, not just figuratively but in reality. We say this not as an easy way of inflating our denominational statistics. (It would be better to leave them out of the figures, because they would only accuse us and increase our responsibility, rather than make us look more important.) We say it for Christ's glory, because His word compels us. No founder of any religion identified himself with the poor as Jesus did. In fact, some of them identified with the rich, presenting wealth rather than poverty as the sign of divine favor, even though impressing on the rich the duty of helping the poor by almsgiving. No one else has said: "Just as you did this to one of the least of these of my brothers or sisters, you did it to me" (Mt 25:40), and here (as everyone agrees) the "least brother or sister" means not only those who believe in Christ, but every person.

The consequence of all this is that the Pope, as Christ's Vicar, really is the "father of the poor," the shepherd of this vast flock. And there is reason to rejoice and thank God that today this is literally true: his is the most authoritative voice raised in their defence, in every part of the world. He is the voice of those who have no voice, and this is recognized outside the Church itself, even by eminent leaders of other religions.

3. The poor to be loved, assisted and evangelized

One last point remains for us to look at briefly, but it is the most important one as far as the poor are concerned: how are we to put our interest in them into practice? How can we give real, as opposed to notional, substance to the "preferential option for the poor" we hear so much about today? The truth is, the poor do not need our good feelings; they need action. Good feelings alone would only serve to lull our guilty conscience. What we specifically need to do for the poor can be summed up in three words: we must love them, assist them and evangelize them.

Love the poor: Love of the poor is one of the most common features of Catholic sanctity. For some saints — St. Vincent de Paul, for example — it actually became the way to holiness. Through the communion of saints, we can begin to ask them to obtain for us a new love and sensitivity towards the poor, so that we love Christ in the poor, and the poor in Christ. As we know, love of Christ and love of the poor are both necessary: the one calls for the other. Some people, such as Charles de Foucauld, arrived at love for the poor by starting with love for Christ. Others, such as Simone Weil, began with love for poor and ordinary people, and this led them to love for Christ.[10]

Loving the poor means first of all respecting them and recognizing their dignity. In them, precisely because they lack other incidental titles and distinctions, the radical dignity of being human shines out more brightly than ever. "In the light of Christ, a complete vision of human life sees more in the poor person than just someone in need. It sees a brother mysteriously invested with a dignity that calls for reverence, a welcoming concern and a compassion beyond what is merely deserved."[11]

This dignity of the poor must be respected above all in the Church, in our assemblies and institutions. There has to be a place in this world where they can truly feel at home, welcomed and not just tolerated. It is so easy, unfortunately, to fail in this elementary duty. St. James said to the first Christians: "Suppose a rich man comes into your synagogue, well dressed and with a gold ring on, and at the same time a poor man comes in dressed in shabby clothes, and you take notice of the well-dressed man and say: 'Come this way to the best seats'; then you tell the poor man: 'Stand over there' or 'You can sit on the floor by my foot rest,' aren't you doing the exact opposite of God? In fact, God chose the poor of this world to make them rich, while you on the other hand despise the poor and choose the rich" (cf. Jm 2:16).

Loving the poor means asking their forgiveness. Forgiveness for failing to reach out to them fully and joyfully, and perpetuating the distance between us and them. Forgiveness for our passive indignation in the face of injustice, and the political slogans we use to talk about them, each of us having our say in an effort to justify our own untroubled existence. Forgiveness for always expecting mathematical certainty that we are not being conned before making any gesture towards them. Forgiveness for not recognizing in them the living tabernacle of the poor and despised Christ. Forgiveness for not being one of them ourselves.

However, the poor deserve not only our sympathy and compassion: they also deserve our admiration. They are humanity's true champions. Every year, the Nobel prize is awarded, and cups and medals of gold, silver and bronze are given out for merit or for winning a race. Someone may have managed to run a distance in a shorter time than someone else, or jump a centimeter higher or win a marathon. Every year the list of the most bizarre and pointless records gets longer. No one, as far as I know, has ever awarded a prize to the poor. And yet if we could only observe the prowess and endurance they are capable of, not just on a single occasion but for a lifetime, the performances of the greatest athletes would seem child's play by comparison. What is a marathon compared to the achievements of a rickshaw man in Calcutta? By the end of his life he has covered the equivalent of several journeys around the world, on foot and in exhausting heat, pulling one or two corpulent passengers along rough roads, over potholes and puddles and darting between cars to avoid being run over.

I wonder if, just as there is a peace prize, it might not be a good idea to institute a poverty prize. Not, obviously, to encourage people to be poor, or start odious competitions between the poor, but to give recognition to what poor people are capable of achieving despite their poverty: their hidden acts of heroism, their incredible patience, and the moving acts of solidarity that often cast the world of the poor in the purest light of sheer humanity, despite all the material and moral misery that can also be found there.

Assist the poor. Our duty is also to assist the poor, as well as to love and respect them. Here again St. James comes to our aid. What is the point, he asks, of feeling sorry for a brother or sister without food or clothing, and saying to them: "You poor thing, you're really suffering! Keep warm, and eat plenty," if you don't give them what they need to eat and warm themselves? Like faith, compassion without works is dead (cf. Jm 2:15-17). At the judgment, Christ will not say: "I was naked and you felt sorry for me," but "I was naked and you clothed me." That is why I think it's a fine thing that a small space has been set aside within the Vatican itself, where the poor can be welcomed and fed and clothed. It's a sign.

We must not blame God for the misery in the world, but ourselves. One day, a man saw a young girl trembling with cold and crying with hunger. He was seized with a sudden fit of revulsion and cried out: "Oh God, where are you? Why don't you do something for that innocent creature?" But an inner voice replied: "I have done something — I created you!" And at once he understood.

Today, however, mere almsgiving is not enough. Thanks to the new possibilities in the field of communication, the problem of poverty has become worldwide. When the Fathers of the Church talked about poverty they were thinking of the poor in their own cities, or at most in the neighboring town. They hardly knew anything else except very vaguely. In any case, even if they had known, it would have been even more difficult to provide aid in an economy like theirs. It is understandable then that Chrysostom, calculating the number of rich and poor in the Constantinople of his day, was able to draw up a plan which he thought would permanently solve the problem of poverty by almsgiving alone.

Today we know that this is not enough, even though nothing can dispense us from doing what we can even on the individual level. We need not go to the lengths of taking up arms to fight injustice with violence (that would immediately put us outside Christ's way), but we can see from the example of so many men and women of our times — such as Dom Helder Camara, Abbé Pierre, Marcello Candia and many others — that much can be done to aid the poor and raise their lifestyle, according to our own means and possibilities. A person might be called to employ cultural resources to benefit the poor, or business acumen or the political power or prestige he or she enjoys. One important expression of this being "for the poor" has certainly been the flourishing liberation theology of Latin America, despite the limitations that have marked it in some cases.

Speaking in *Evangelica testificatio* of the "cry of the poor," Paul VI said to religious in particular: "It leads some of you to join the poor in their situation and to share their bitter cares. Furthermore, it calls many of your Institutes to rededicate some of their works for the good of the poor."[12]

What we need today is a new crusade, a mass mobilization of all Christians, indeed of the whole civilized world, to liberate those living tombs of Christ who are the millions upon millions of people dying of hunger, disease and want. That would be a crusade worthy of the name — worthy of Christ's cross. We should rejoice and thank God that this crusade is already under way, at least to a small extent, through the efforts of so many individuals, institutions, parish and religious communities and humanitarian associations. And, for those with eyes to see, there is also today a "Peter the Hermit" travelling the world encouraging everyone to join the crusade. I mean the Pope.

The elimination or reduction of the unjust and scandalous abyss that exists between rich and poor in the world is the most urgent, most enormous task that the closing millennium entrusts to the new century.

Evangelize the poor. Finally, after loving and aiding the poor comes evangelization. Jesus recognized this as His own mission par excellence (cf. Lk 4:18) which He entrusted to His Church. We must not let our guilty conscience lead us to commit the enormous injustice of withholding the good news from those who are its first and most natural recipients, possibly with the excuse that, as the proverb says "a hungry belly has no ears."

Jesus multiplied the loaves and the Word together; in fact He first administered the Word, sometimes for three days on end, and then worried about the loaves as well. The poor man does not live on bread alone but also on hope, and on every word that comes from God's mouth. The poor have the inviolable right to hear the Gospel in its entirety, not a reduced, conveniently adapted edition.

Even today, they have the right to hear the good news that "blessed are you poor." Yes, blessed in spite of everything, because there is an immense "possibility" open to you which is closed to the rich, or at least very difficult for them: namely, the Kingdom. Certainly, to actually possess the Kingdom requires belief in the Gospel, or at least, for those with no possibility of knowing the Gospel, a life of moral goodness and honesty according to the dictates of one's own religion or conscience. But aren't you already fortunate and blessed to have the possibility open before you, if all it takes is your decision to make it a reality? Human beings — according to a certain modern philosophy — are only "possibilities," they are as rich as the wealth of possibilities they enjoy. You who are poor possess the one possibility that contains all other possibilities, without which all the others are nothing at all.

We conclude by recalling the two main sayings of God that have guided our way: "Blessed the man who is concerned for the poor!" These words are immediately followed in the psalm by a promise used in the liturgy in the form of a prayer "For the Supreme Pontiff": "The Lord will protect him and give him life; he will bless him on earth and save him from the hands of his enemies."[13]

This promise is not just for the Pope but for every pastor, and for all who decide to take the cause of the poor to heart. Christ turned this promise from an earthly one into a heavenly one, from a temporal one into an eternal one, when He revealed what He would say on the last day to those who have been concerned for the poor: "Come, you blessed by my Father! Inherit the kingdom prepared for you from the foundation of the world" (Mt 25:34).

II

"He became poor for your sake"

Material Poverty:
AN EVANGELICAL PROPOSITION TO BE EMBRACED

1. Being "for the poor" and being "poor"

In the matter of poverty, too, the transition from the Old to the New Testament marks a qualitative leap which can be summarized thus: the Old Testament introduces us to a God who is "for the poor," while the New Testament shows us a God who Himself becomes poor. The Old Testament is full of passages about God who "listens to the cry of the poor," who "shows pity to the poor and the weak" and "gives justice to the oppressed."[1] Only the Gospel tells us about God who makes Himself one of them, choosing weakness and poverty for Himself: "Though He was rich, Jesus Christ became poor for your sake" (2 Cor 8:9).

From being an evil to be avoided, material poverty takes on the aspect of something good that is to be cultivated, an ideal to be pursued. Here is the great innovation brought by Christ. The Old Testament was familiar with what we have termed *negative material poverty*, that is, poverty as a social reality to be combated or avoided. It also knew *positive spiritual poverty*, at least from a certain period onwards — in other words, the ideal of people who trust in God alone. Lastly, it was familiar with the *negative spiritual poverty* of those who are rich in things and goods but poor in wisdom, which is true wealth. I repeat, it knew nothing of *positive material poverty* that could be freely chosen. Even the poverty practiced at Qumran among the Essenes was not, in itself, a choice of material poverty. Rather, as in the early Christian community at Jerusalem, it was a pooling of goods "so that there would be no one in need among them" (cf. Dt 15:4; Ac 4:34). It may also have been dictated by a concern to ensure the ritual purity of the group by eliminating all need for contact with the outside world of the "impure."

In this way the two essential components of the ideal of biblical poverty are now made clear: to be "for the poor" and to "be poor." The history of Christian poverty is the story of the different attitudes adopted towards these two demands. This is reflected, for example, in the different ways of interpreting the episode of the rich young man (cf. Mt 19:16 ff.). Sometimes the "sell everything" aspect of the story is stressed, at other times the "give to the poor" aspect. In other words, sometimes the accent is placed on emptying oneself in order to follow

Christ radically, and sometimes on concern for the poor.[2]

In ancient times the interpretation of the Encratites — a radical movement advocating total abstinence (*engrateia*) from marriage and possessions — was countered by the conciliatory view of people like Clement of Alexandria. He almost went to the opposite extreme when he said that what counted was not poverty so much as the use one made of riches: "Those who consider possessions, gold, silver and houses as God's gifts, and honor the giver by using their possessions to share in the work of salvation of others, are the ones who are declared blessed by the Lord and proclaimed poor in spirit."[3]

An early synthesis and balance between the two positions was achieved in the thought of men like Saint Basil and Saint Augustine and in the forms of monastic life they started. The latter combined the most rigorous personal poverty with an equal concern for the poor and the sick, embodied in special institutions which in some cases served as models for the future charitable work of the Church.

In the Middle Ages, the same cycle was repeated in a different context. The Church, and in particular the ancient monastic Orders which in the West had grown very rich, now cultivated poverty almost exclusively in the form of assistance to the poor and to pilgrims, in other words by running charitable relief programs. From the early 1100's onwards, the so-called poverty movements arose to counter this situation. They placed the effective practice of poverty in the forefront, advocating a return by the Church to the simplicity and poverty of the Gospel. This time the balance and synthesis were achieved by the mendicant Orders, which strove to combine radical detachment with loving care for the poor, lepers and slaves, and above all to live their poverty in communion with the Church, not in opposition to it.

With all due caution we can perhaps detect a similar dialectic in the modern era as well. The outbreak of a social conscience in the last century and the problem of the working class once again upset the balance and led to the eclipse of the ideal of voluntary poverty chosen and lived as a way of following Christ, while interest shifted to the problem of the poor. The ideal of a poor Church was eclipsed by concern "for the poor," translated into a thousand new initiatives and institutions, especially in the area of education of poor children and assistance to those most neglected. The Church's social teaching is also a product of this spiritual climate.

It was Vatican II, especially following the famous intervention by Cardinal Lercaro, that brought the topic of "the Church and poverty" back to center stage. The Constitution on the Church has this to say on the matter: "Just as Christ carried out the work of redemption in poverty and oppression, so the Church is called to follow the same path... Christ was sent by the Father to bring the good news to the poor… to heal the contrite of heart, to seek and save what was lost. Similarly, the Church encompasses with her love all those who are afflicted by human misery, and she recognizes in those who are poor and who suffer the image of her poor and suffering Founder. She does all in her power to relieve their need and in them she strives to serve Christ."[4]

In this text both aspects are combined: being poor and being at the service of the poor. The catechesis of Pope John Paul II on poverty, given at a Wednesday audience after the Synod of Bishops on the Religious Life, highlights the same two elements: "The Church feels ever more strongly the impulse of the Spirit to be poor among the poor, to remind everyone of the need to conform to the ideal of poverty preached and practiced by Christ, and to imitate Him in His sincere and active love for the poor."[5]

However, these two aspects are not necessarily to be cultivated in equal measure by every believer or by every category of believers. We must also keep in mind the teaching about charisms and the different functions assigned to each member of Christ's body. St. Paul seems to include in his list of charisms the voluntary giving up of one's goods for the sake of others. In fact for him, "giving with simplicity" is a charism (cf. Rm 12:6 ff.). "Giving away all one's wealth to the poor" is a charism, just as, in the same context, are prophecy, speaking in tongues and knowledge (cf. 1 Cor 13:3 ff.). This shows us once again that the traditional category of a "counsel" is insufficient by itself to explain the evangelical proposal of chastity and poverty. A person who has received a gift does not have the same freedom to respond to it or not, as someone who has received a counsel. Furthermore, a charism does not create divisions, or categories of more perfect and less perfect. It creates responsibility rather than superiority.

Therefore the Church, in some of its members, gives greater expression to the poor Christ, in others to the Christ who takes on Himself the "infirmities and diseases" of the poor (cf. Mt 8:17). The fullness of the Spirit and His gifts resides in the Church, not in the individual believer; but that fullness, in the communion of the Church, becomes the property of all. If in fact I love unity and remain in union with it, then whatever each person has or does within that unity also belongs to me and is done by me. I belong to that body which is poor and which takes care of the poor. "Banish envy" — said Saint Augustine — "and what is mine will be yours, and if I banish envy what is yours will be mine."[6]

The consequence of this is that we need to banish animosity and judgment and substitute mutual esteem and rejoicing over the good that God accomplishes through others. Those who work for social justice and the advancement of the poor (often needing large-scale resources and structures) are happy that there are others who live and proclaim the Gospel in poverty and simplicity, and vice versa. "Let us stop passing judgment on one another" was the Apostle's exhortation in a similar situation, "and seek instead the ways that lead to peace and mutual support" (cf. Rm 14:13, 19).

2. Renewal of poverty "in the Spirit"

Having spoken in the previous chapter about the duty to be "for the poor," we can now turn our attention to the need to be poor.

I said that positive material poverty is what constitutes the originality of the Gospel. We must now be specific about how this is true. Saint Thomas wrote that "even the moral precepts contained in the Gospel would be dead letters that kill, unless the healing grace of faith were added to them."[7] So, even the beatitudes would have remained a dead letter if Jesus had merely confined Himself to proclaiming them on the mountain. The greatest innovation therefore lies not so much in the fact that Jesus commands things that are more perfect than the old law, as in the grace He has acquired for us to put them into practice. "The new law" — St. Thomas concludes — "is principally the grace of the Holy Spirit Himself."[8] In other words, the prophecy of Ezekiel has come true: "I will put my spirit within you, and make you follow my statutes, and be careful to observe my ordinances" (Ezk 36:27). This means: "I will put my Spirit within you, and that will enable you to observe my laws and put them into practice." The beatitudes, like the precepts and the so-called evangelical counsels, are also a new law, but in the *material sense,* in other words new in their content, while the grace of the Holy Spirit is a new law in the *formal* or *causal sense*, because it gives the capacity to put into practice what the laws prescribe.

It follows from this that every plan or effort to renew poverty in the Church in the way the Council envisaged cannot come about except "in the Holy Spirit." On the occasion of the sixteenth centenary of the Ecumenical Council of Constantinople in 1981, John Paul II wrote: "The whole work of *renewing the Church*, which Vatican II so providentially proposed and initiated, can only come about *in the Holy Spirit,* in other words with the help of His light and His energy."[9] Any attempt at renewal that leaves out this vital aspect is doomed to failure.

Wherein lies the difference between renewal "in law" and renewal "in the Spirit"? Positive law, being external to human beings, does not change the state of their hearts. It does not give people the ability to fulfill what it prescribes. In a word, it does not "give life" (cf. Gal 3:21). It pushes a person to do or to avoid something *by coercion*, under threat of punishment or blame. It is based on fear.

The interior law, on the other hand, which is the Holy Spirit Himself (cf. Rm 8:2), changes the heart; it not only indicates the will of another, but is a new principle, active and operative. It not only commands you to do something, but helps you to do it. It creates that new heart which willingly does the things God commands because it loves God and trusts Him. It is based on love and moves a person to act *by attraction*.

All this is particularly true of poverty, which Christ never presented as a "law," but as a "counsel," or rather as a "beatitude," that is, as something that draws you through the promise of happiness: "Everyone is attracted by the object of their desire."[10] The Holy Spirit is able to renew the evangelical ideal of poverty in the Church, by infusing a love for poverty. More precisely: by infusing *Christ's* love for poverty, because when we speak of the Holy Spirit we are actually talking about the Spirit "of Jesus."

We need to ask the Holy Spirit to make us fall in love with poverty, because any lover of poverty will easily find ways and means of practicing it. Without this, the best efforts of laws, canons, monastic rules and constitutions to draft the most beautiful and plausible frameworks for poverty, will all remain a dead letter. All they do is make our sinfulness apparent, in other words they highlight the gulf that exists between what we ought to be and what in fact we are, which is exactly what the Law did before Christ (cf. Rm 7:7). The history of Christian spirituality, especially of the religious Orders, stands as proof that the Church's poverty was never renewed by multiplying laws. At best, they managed to check some of the more glaring abuses, or slow the rate of decline. In general, the more actual poverty declines, the more laws there are about it. But the laws themselves can easily turn spiritual poverty legalistic and pharisaical.

It is enough to think of what religious poverty had become at certain periods, despite the multiplication of canons and laws. One small example of this: according to canon law and the Constitutions, if a religious was on a journey he was allowed, even obliged, to accept anything that people might offer him on the way, since every offering automatically belonged to the community. But he did not have the right to give anything to anyone, not even alms to a poor person, since he owned nothing himself. Here was a form of poverty that only allowed you to receive, never to give! We know from Jesus that by the same process, that is by declaring one's possessions "a sacred offering made to the Temple," the Pharisees prevented their disciples even from assisting their father and mother, thus abolishing the commandment of God (cf. Mk 7:11 ff.).

Someone has summarized the spirit of the old Code in matters of poverty as follows: "prudent management of the economy, wise capitalization and secure bank accounts."[11] Poverty was, and largely still is, reduced to dependence on superiors in the use of goods and money. It was and is only individual poverty, in the sense that the individual has "nothing of his or her own," not a poverty that is also communal and collective. Today, on the other hand, everyone would admit that it is wrong to call oneself poor when one belongs to a rich community.

Paradoxically, the only laws that have succeeded in drastically bringing about poverty among religious (we say this with sadness and embarrassment) have been civil laws, those of the State. A religious missionary sister said: "After the Council we had discussed for years how to renew our poverty, but we never came to any conclusions. Then a Marxist regime came to power in the country and took everything away from us. It did, at a stroke, what we had been unable to do by ourselves." It is obvious, though, that this is not the kind of poverty we want and need.

The periodical real renewals of poverty in the Church have always come about "in the Spirit," thanks to a renewed and intense contact with the person of Jesus and His Gospel. There is an ever-burning flame present throughout history, and it is the Spirit of the risen Jesus. From this flame comes the spark that each time rekindles the ideal of poverty in the Church. Therefore, as far as poverty is concerned, we need to go back to this original source from time to time, without stopping at any intermediary source, not even that of our own religious founder. However rich they may be, the particular sources of a religious Institute are not "living and enduring." Being historical and partial embodiments they are linked to a particular context and situation, and we know how decisive one's cultural and economic context is in the matter of poverty. A good example of what I am saying was given by the Pope at the Wednesday audience I mentioned earlier. He was talking about something which has even given its name to a whole series of religious Orders: the mendicant Orders. "In the past," the Pope said, "it was possible to choose mendicancy as a sign of poverty, humility and charity towards the needy. Today it is rather by means of their work that religious acquire what they need to support themselves and their activities."[12]

Historical forms of poverty through the centuries, precisely because they are contingent, are many and varied. Poverty can be eremitical, cenobitical (either Pachomian, Basilian or Benedictine), Franciscan, apostolic or proper to Clerks Regular, and so forth. Besides, even if it were possible for Rules to indicate the way of poverty once and for all, they would still have achieved almost nothing, because Rules alone cannot provide, along with knowledge about the way, the strength to follow it. Paraphrasing John's Gospel, we have to say "the law was given through the Founders (Basil, Benedict, Francis, etc.), but grace has come through Jesus Christ" (cf. Jn 1:17). Religious Rules and Founders play their finest role when they constantly refer us back each time to Jesus and his Gospel. "I have done what was mine to do," Francis of Assisi said as he was approaching his death; "May Christ teach you what you are to do."[13] Whenever we stop short at Rules and Founders we unwittingly change them into barriers between us and Christ, rather than channels. This happens with postulants and novices, and generally in the formation of the young, whenever we immediately start talking about the charism of the Founder and the spirituality of our Institute, devoting most of the novitiate, retreats and renewal courses to these matters without having first given them a solid formation in the things that are essential for everyone: knowledge of Christ, familiarity with God's Word and with the action of the Holy Spirit.

We must therefore go back to the source of all sources. "Behind the bridegroom, the bride looks attractive,"[14] said Dante, referring to Francis and Lady Poverty. But how much truer is that line if by Bridegroom we understand Jesus Christ Himself, rather than Francis, His follower! Behind Jesus, on his arm, poverty too is pleasing and beautiful. It is the only way it has of being pleasing and loveable. We need, then, to go back upstream along the great river of poverty, and return to its source, without stopping at any of its waterfalls or intervening weirs.

3. Poverty in the life of Christ

The Acts of the Apostles tell us about "all that Jesus did and taught from the beginning" (Ac 1:1). He first practiced what He later taught. So let us now look at His life as a poor man, and then go on to consider His teaching about poverty.

This time too we shall use two words as beacons to light up our way. The first, introducing us to the lived poverty of Christ, is well known: "Although (Christ) was rich, yet for your sakes He became poor, so that by His poverty you might become rich" (2 Cor 8:9). There is no doubt that this refers to the material poverty of Christ. The meaning is: Christ, being (or having it in His power to be) rich, became *materially* poor in order to enrich us *spiritually*. St. Thomas comments: "He endured material poverty in order to give us spiritual riches."[15] He did not come to make people richer in worldly goods, but to make them God's children and heirs to eternal life.

Many have noted the parallelism that exists between this text and the Christological hymn in the Letter to the Philippians, especially between the expression "He became poor" (*eptocheusen*) and "He emptied Himself" (*ekenosen*). Christ's poverty is clearly an aspect of His *kenosis*, His self-abasement, in the Incarnation. In its structure, the phrase also recalls the passage that says that Christ "became a victim for sin, so that in Him we might become the righteousness of God" (cf. 2 Cor 5:21).

Christ's poverty has, first of all, a concrete existential aspect that accompanies Him from birth to death. Blessed Angela of Foligno has a very profound passage about this aspect of the Savior's poverty: "Christ's poverty was of three kinds: Christ, the way, the guide of our souls, exemplified the first degree of the most perfect poverty by choosing to live poorly and to be poor, bereft of all earthly possessions. He kept nothing for Himself: no house, vineyard, coins, money, estate, dish ware, or any other possessions. He neither accepted any earthly goods, nor wanted to accept anything but a life of extreme bodily neediness, with scarcity, hunger, thirst, cold, hard labor, austerity and hardship... The second degree of poverty, greater than the first, was that He wished to be poor with regard to relatives, friends and all earthly affections... The third and supreme degree of poverty was that Christ stripped Himself of His very self, became poor with regard to His own power, wisdom and glory."[16] Jesus, then, was poor in things, poor in supports and poor in prestige.

This third type of poverty is the most profound of all because it goes beyond the level of possessions and touches the sphere of being. For Christ, this consisted in the very fact of becoming man, of divesting Himself, if not of His divine nature, at least of everything which that nature could have claimed for itself in terms of glory, wealth and splendor. "Is there any greater poverty for God," exclaims St.

Gregory of Nyssa, "than the form of a slave? Is there a greater humiliation than to share in our nature?"[17] In Christ, poverty shines out in its most sublime form: not in the fact of *being* poor (which can be an imposed or inherited state), but of *becoming* poor, and becoming so out of love, in order to enrich others.

However, some common assumptions about Christ's material poverty may need correction on the basis of a more careful examination of the Gospels. As far as we can ascertain, Jesus did not belong, sociologically speaking, to the proletarian or lowest class of His day. He was a craftsman who earned His living by His own work, which was certainly a better condition than that of a dependent worker. Even during His lifetime, the prestige attending Him as a rabbi, the invitations He received even from well-off people, the friendships He enjoyed (like those of Lazarus and his sisters), the help He received from a few rich women (cf. Lk 8:2 ff.) — these factors prevent us from seeing Him as the poorest of the poor. Even the phrase: "Foxes have their dens and the birds of the air their nests, but the Son of Man has nowhere to lay His head" (Lk 9:58), makes sense in view of His condition as a wandering preacher with no fixed abode, rather than indicating that He had nowhere to live, though that meaning may be included.

From the strictly material point of view, there were certainly people in His day who were poorer than He was, entire masses of the disinherited, for whom He Himself felt compassion when He saw them "harassed and helpless" (Mt 9:36). Even His future disciples, for example certain ascetics and hermits of the desert, included some who exceeded their Master in terms of austerity and purely material poverty.

The misunderstanding arises from attributing excessive value to the external, material *manifestations* of poverty. Jesus never claimed preeminence in poverty, as He did in charity when He said that no one could have greater love than to lay down one's life for his friends (cf. Jn 15:13). He was free even in relation to His poverty, just as He freely ate and drank to the point of being taken for a drunkard and a glutton. John the Baptist was much more rigid in terms of asceticism than He was. Jesus never fell into the trap some of His imitators later fell into, of making material poverty absolute, using it as a measure of perfection and ending up being rich in the worst thing there is: in themselves and their own justice. There are no absolutes where material things are concerned, no point beyond which it is impossible to go. However much one may want to be poor, one will always find someone poorer. Material poverty is a bottomless pit.

Let us rather turn our attention to the *reasons* for Christ's poverty, why He became poor. The meaning of His choice is revealed for us in what the Apostle says at the beginning of the first Letter to the Corinthians: "Since in the wisdom of God the world was unable to recognize God through wisdom, God decided to save those who believe through the foolishness of our proclamation" (1 Cor 1:21). In other words: since the world did not recognize and honor God when He revealed Himself through creation, in splendor, power, wisdom and wealth, so He has now decided to save fallen humanity by the opposite means: through poverty, weakness, humility and foolishness. He has decided to reveal Himself "in the guise of His opposite" in order to challenge human pride and wisdom.

What is denied in this way is not the goodness of creation and of all the good things it comprises, but the sinful component contributed by human beings. As we would say today, the superstructure rather than the structure. In the Incarnation, the Word does not limit itself to assuming human nature in order to raise it as it is. Rather, it challenges, corrects and straightens out that nature, revealing the inner corruption which had come to overlay it. In this way, Christian discourse about renunciation of one's wealth, body and will — in other words, about the evangelical counsels of poverty, chastity and obedience — stands on a level of its own, different from that of any other religion and philosophy with a dualistic background.

Whenever Christ's self-emptying is mentioned there is always a reference to what happened in Adam, through sin. Christ "did not regard equality with God as something to be grasped" (cf. Ph 2:6) as Adam had done. Humanity therefore had to divest itself of what had been plundered from God: of its own self-will first of all, and then of the goods to which, once having strayed from God, it had avidly turned. Through poverty, a kind of return takes place to the original state in which people *possess* nothing while *enjoying* everything, have nothing of their own, yet all is theirs because their "social love" has not yet turned into "private love" that wants everything for itself.[18]

As well as what we might call this negative reason for God's choice of poverty, St. Paul himself brings out another, which is the positive reason of love: "He became poor for your sakes, so that by His poverty you might become rich" (2 Cor 8:9). A gift is most precious when it is the result of self-denial, when the giver deprives himself of what is given. And the Word in some sense deprived Himself of His divine wealth in order to share it with us. God's poverty is an expression of His *agape*, of the fact that He is love. The profound meaning of St. Paul's words is revealed in what he says elsewhere: "Christ loved us and gave Himself up for us" (cf. Eph 5:2).

4. "Blessed are you poor!"

Moving from Jesus' life to His *teaching* about poverty, we immediately meet the other key saying of this meditation: "How blessed are you who are poor: the Kingdom of God is yours!" (Lk 6: 20). We know that Luke stresses real or material poverty more than spiritual, though the latter is obviously present in his Gospel.

Let us go straight to the core of Christ's message, to the motive for such an unprecedented beatitude. This is unmistakable and clearly expressed in the text: namely, the Kingdom of God. We can apply to those who are voluntarily poor the same words that Christ applies to eunuchs (cf. Mt 19:12): there are some who are poor from birth, others have been made so by people, and others again have made themselves that way for the sake of the Kingdom of Heaven.

It is at once clear why the ideal of material poverty and of perfect chastity make their appearance in history only at this moment, with Christ. The reason is that only with Him has God's Kingdom, their sole justification, come onto the scene. The Kingdom has ushered in a new age, the age of redemption or of "the return of creatures to God," following that of creation or "the departure of creatures from God." The Kingdom creates an alternative, a new possibility in the world: earthly goods and even marriage itself are no longer the only choice or value. From now on, there exists another way which, far from nullifying the old ones, makes them relative. They appear as what they truly are, provisional realities destined to disappear in the new world. The same thing happens with the idea of the State in the political sphere: Caesar's kingdom is not abolished by the simultaneous presence of God's Kingdom in history, but is rendered radically relative. The former kingdom is no longer absolute in its own sphere.

However, we need to see how this motive works in practice—in other words, why it is that the Kingdom justifies and demands poverty. Here I must repeat, in part, what I wrote on another occasion with reference to virginity. Everything draws its meaning from the *nature* of this Kingdom: it is "already" present in the world, but "not yet" fully and finally established.

Since the Kingdom of God is already present on earth in the person and preaching of Jesus, we must not let it elude us, but must grasp it, giving up anything that might stand in its way, even a hand or an eye if necessary (cf. Mt 18:8 ff.). In other words, it is possible even now to begin living in the way that will be normal once the Kingdom is finally established, when earthly goods will have lost all value, and God will be all in all.

This is what we might call the *eschatological*, or *prophetic*, motivation for poverty, in the sense that it proclaims the new heaven and the new earth. Poverty is prophetic because detachment from earthly goods is a silent, but effective, proclamation that other riches exist. It reminds us that the world as we know it is passing away, that we have no abiding dwelling place here below, but that our homeland is in heaven. It affirms the primacy of the spirit over matter, of the invisible over what is seen, of eternity over time.

The best illustration of this eschatological motivation is provided by the parables of the hidden treasure and the pearl of great price. "The Kingdom of Heaven is like treasure hidden in a field which someone has found... he goes off joyfully, sells everything he owns and buys the field" (cf. Mt 13:44 ff.). Christ does not say: "A man sold all his possessions and set out to find a hidden treasure." If someone came and told us that, we would immediately think that this was one of the many deluded people one occasionally comes across, who set out in search of some elusive hidden treasure and end up losing everything they had, but finding nothing. No! Jesus says that the man sold everything, not in order to look for treasure, but because he had found it. Poverty is not the price we must pay in return for the Kingdom. It is the effect, not the cause, of the Kingdom's arrival.

How simple these two images are: the treasure and the pearl! Yet Christ uses them to set the hearts of many ablaze with love for poverty. They constantly reappear in the history of famous conversions: Augustine says in his *Confessions*, "I had now found the precious pearl, and needed to sell all I had in order to acquire it."[19] These are parables which, once their message has been heard, have a quite special ability to bring us to crisis point, leaving us no longer content with our own mediocrity. They give us a glimpse of the "wondrous exchange," the opportunity of a lifetime. They exercise a fascination, they really do work "by attraction"! All their power remains intact, which means that even now, were they to find one of us whose heart was ready to be "grasped," ready to take them seriously, as we would with an invitation personally addressed to us by Christ, they could quite easily produce one of those conversions we talked about — even today.

This eschatological motivation, based on the sudden breaking in of the Kingdom — or, after Easter, on the expectation of the imminent return of Christ — continued to operate subsequently, but in a slightly different way. For the Christian, earthly citizenship is not permanent; he or she belongs to another city. This is why it makes no sense to be attached to the goods of the present time, which may have to be left behind at any moment. The eschatological motivation is now active in the form of *hope* for those good things which are eternal.

It was in this context that the famous ideal of "flight from the world" arose, by which the Christian in some way anticipates his departure from this present world. St. Bernard has an exhortation along the same lines: "Be resolute," he says, "in leaving aside all greed. The things of this world are to be despised, not insofar as they are given to us to be used, but insofar as they cause the ruin of many people. It is hard for someone to run if they are weighed down by heavy burdens. A free person on the other hand runs faster and more surely. We must free ourselves of the heavy baggage of earthly possessions, so as to struggle with the devil unhindered, for he is stark in his power. Try to have nothing that could slow you down: you must shake off anything that could hold you back as you hasten towards your homeland... We need to embrace spiritual poverty. Let anyone who wants to live a godly life remember that nature arranges compensation for the lack of great wealth. The road is short; there is no need to bring too many things for the journey."[20]

So much for the first characteristic of the Kingdom, namely, that it has *already* come. Since, however, there is a sense in which the Kingdom has *not yet* arrived, but is still on the way until it "reaches the ends of the earth," there is a need for people who devote themselves entirely to its coming, who are free of all other earthly bonds and commitments that might be an obstacle to such a proclamation. If the Gospel is to reach "to the ends of the earth" (Ac 1:8), then its messengers, like athletes in a race, need to be light, free and unhindered, so that "the word of the Lord may spread rapidly" (cf. 2 Th 3:1). This is the second motivation for poverty, which we might call *missionary* or *apostolic*, and is particularly highlighted in the "missionary discourses" of Jesus: "Take nothing for your journey, no staff, nor bag, nor bread, nor money — not even an extra tunic" (Lk 9:3).

This tells us that Christ's teaching contains two different levels or forms of poverty: one required of everyone in order to *enter* the Kingdom, the other required of a few in particular in order to *announce* the Kingdom. This second and more radical demand Jesus makes to those He calls to share in His work of proclaiming the Kingdom and being totally devoted to its cause: the apostles, that small group of disciples who followed Him on a full-time basis. The radical demand addressed to the rich young man should certainly be interpreted in this sense. Christ was not only inviting him to be converted to the Gospel, but also to stay with Him, to become in some sense an apostle. The invitation addressed to him is very similar to that addressed to Matthew (cf. Mt 9:9).

It is this form of poverty that eventually evolved — after some profound adaptations — into the various forms of religious poverty in the Church. One author writes: "The group of disciples around Jesus can be considered as the prototype of life according to the evangelical counsels in the Church."[21]

One shining example of this apostolic poverty, undertaken with a view to proclaiming the Gospel, is found at the origins of the mendicant Orders, especially the Friars Preachers, or Dominicans. At a certain point during the struggle against the

Albigensians and Cathars, it became clear that the repeated failures of the Church were due to the poverty and detachment of the heretical preachers, in stark contrast to the wealth and worldliness of the Catholic clergy. People paid more attention to personal witness than to orthodoxy of doctrine, sometimes even throwing stones to drive away preachers who arrived in the villages on horseback, splendidly attired. It was then that the Spirit raised up men like Dominic Guzman and Francis of Assisi, who made the Church's proclamation effective once more by restoring the apostolic form of life in poverty.

5. "We have found the truly poor man!"

Now, continuing our efforts to shed light on the real motivation behind evangelical poverty, we need to go one step further. In the New Testament, we observe the same phenomenon with respect to voluntary poverty as in relation to chastity for the Kingdom. In the text of Matthew 19 the motive for celibacy is termed "the Kingdom of heaven"; in 1 Corinthians 7, which deals with virgins, it is called "the Lord": "The unmarried man is anxious about the affairs of the Lord, how to please the Lord." The same happens with poverty. Even in this case the mention of the Kingdom becomes rarer and rarer, and gives way to the person of Christ. The reason for this is that Jesus Christ, who died and is risen, is now

God's new way of reigning. "God reigns from the wood of the cross" (*Regnavit a ligno Deus*), as the Church began to say very early on, adapting a verse of a psalm (cf. Ps 96:10). In Christ, poverty also is seated on the throne,

> "and so, while Mary stayed below,
> she shed her tears, with Christ, upon the Cross."[22]

Poverty has followed Christ even onto the cross. It was here that He really "espoused" poverty. Henceforth one cannot choose the one without the other: neither Christ without poverty, nor poverty without Christ. Poverty has become one aspect of the more general imitation of Christ. It is part and parcel of developing "the same mind in you as was in Christ Jesus" (cf. Ph 2:5). "We have found the truly poor man!" exclaims Saint Augustine. "He is the one who will be found to be a member of this Poor Man."[23] Saint Bernard relies on this mystical principle when he writes: "Any member of Christ's body should be ashamed to make a show of affectation, when his Head is crowned with thorns. Let him understand that such refinements do him no credit, but rather expose him to ridicule."[24]

If we observe the lives of the greatest lovers of poverty in the history of the Church, we see at once that love for Christ — the desire to "follow the naked Christ in nakedness" — as *The Imitation of Christ* says[25] — lies at the heart of everything. Very often, the hidden treasure and the pearl of great price refer to Christ Himself, "in whom are hidden all the treasures of wisdom and knowledge" (Col 2:3). It is no longer a cause, therefore, even the cause of the Kingdom, but a *person*. Such was the poverty lived in recent times by Charles de Foucauld: a "mysticism consisting in the imitation of the poor Christ."[26]

In the light of all this, poverty appears not so much as a virtue or a counsel, or an ascetical ideal, or even only as a charism, but as an intimate sharing in the mystery of the person of Christ, and by that very fact, in the mystery of His Bride, the Church. St. Paul is the one who brings this out most clearly. There is a difference of emphasis in the way St. John presents the mystery of the Incarnation, compared to St. Paul. St. John highlights the *fact*, the ontological aspect of the event. St. Paul brings out the *manner* of the Incarnation, its existential aspect: "He made Himself poor"; "He took on the form of a slave." For him, not only is it important to state that the Word became man, but also what kind of man He became: a poor, humble man, a suffering servant. Indeed, in this he is basing himself on the facts given in the Gospels. The Gospels, in fact, are our evidence for asserting that Christ was born in poverty, lived in greater poverty, and died in extreme poverty.

The Fathers of the Church were especially concerned to underline the first, ontological aspect of the Incarnation, because their culture and also the heresies of the moment (Docetism and Gnosticism) led them to do so. Today, while jealously preserving their achievements, there is also a need to rediscover the value of the Pauline perspective. Patristic Christology was built up almost entirely around John 1:14 ("The Word was made flesh"). There is no trace of what, for Paul, was decisive and in a sense constituted the most revolutionary innovation in the whole economy of redemption. For them, the really important question to ask about Christ's human nature was whether it was complete or incomplete, in other words, endowed with flesh, a soul and a human will. Not that they were unconcerned with the poverty and humility of Christ, but such things did not enter into the definition of His personhood and mystery, except to a minimal extent. They did not — to use their own language — touch upon substance or essence, but only on accidents such as His actions and his existence. They referred, not to the foundations of salvation but only to its accomplishment. Today we are in a position to see that poverty lies at the very heart of the Christian mystery, rather than on its outer edge.

6. "We have left everything and followed you"

We had set ourselves the task of letting the ideal of evangelical poverty, as far as possible, shine before us once again in all its brightness, trusting in the inherent power of attraction it possesses in virtue of Christ who revealed it. There are two moments in the Gospel — reported one after the other as in a diptych — that encourage us in this approach. One does so negatively, by showing us what is lost by not following the ideal; the other positively, by showing us the benefits of doing so.

The rich young man, we read, "went away sad." He had good reason to be. He had been loved by Christ, sought out by Him. He had received from Christ a silent declaration of love, in a single glance: "Looking at him, Jesus loved him" (Mk 10:21). His wealth prevented him from receiving it. By now, he would have been an apostle, remembered by name, together with the others, venerated and loved throughout the centuries. Instead he disappears, without a name, into the night of history.

On the other hand, Peter exclaims: "Look, we have left everything and followed you," and Jesus replies promising a hundredfold in this world, and eternal life (Mk 10:28 ff.). Could any of the apostles at that moment have imagined, even remotely, just how far Jesus' promise would come true for them, literally, in this world? If they had not left everything to follow Christ, they would have remained obscure Galilean fishermen and no one would have known they existed. But now, the whole world is full of their names. The mystery of all this hits me between the eyes every time I walk into St. Peter's Basilica in

Rome and see the people filing past to kiss the foot of the bronze statue of the Apostle.

The important thing for us, however, is to realize that the choice is still open. The living, risen Christ is still walking by and calling people. It is up to us to choose between the two destinies: that of the rich young man or that of the apostles. We too could say with Peter: "Look, we have left everything and followed you," but we know very well that at one level our choice is not yet complete, it still has to be made, or at least renewed. It is not necessarily a case of a spectacular decision, like the first time, one that changes the external circumstances of our life, even though God could ask that of us too. (Not many years ago, He called Cardinal Leger to become a simple missionary in Africa.) It's more a case of giving concrete form and completeness to the choice we once made.

This is where the talk about the law comes in and finds its proper place. "Do we then overthrow the law by faith?" asked the Apostle Paul, and then he replied: "By no means! On the contrary, we uphold the law" (Rm 3:31). The same is true of laws about poverty. Our insistence on renewal "in the Spirit" does not deny the need for laws; rather, it gives them a new foundation and a nobler function. Not that of "bringing sin to light" (cf. Rm 7:7), but that of revealing God's will and plan for me, as the handmaid of grace, not its sterile surrogate.

Let us suppose that at this point, spurred on by

the Spirit, we have fallen in love with evangelical poverty and decided to embrace it with new enthusiasm. However, we do not know exactly what such a choice requires of each of us in practice at the present time. In any case, if we live in a community, we cannot invent our own form of poverty, for our personal use and enjoyment. This is where the law steps in to help us — specifically, canon law if I am an ecclesiastic, and the Rule and Constitutions and my Founder's example, if I am a religious. The law helps me to translate my heart's choice into practice, to discern what God wants of me in the matter of poverty, in my actual situation. But the difference is that now I am attracted, not forced. I no longer see rules, canons, conciliar decrees and statements of the Pope or the Synod of Bishops about religious life as external impositions. Rather, I see all these things as valuable resources to help me keep hold of the treasure I once glimpsed, the pearl of great price. And so I read them, take an interest in them, try to examine my life in the light of them. This actually does happen in communities where love for poverty is alive, whereas in others everything ends in sterile debates and the multiplication of documents. In the former, questions are asked periodically about the best way to cultivate poverty, and members reexamine its practice in their lives.

That is not all. Suppose a young person decides to say yes to Christ's invitation to sell everything and follow Him. This is the moment when a vocation blossoms forth, in many ways similar to falling in love. What does a young person do when he or she falls in love "for real"? They know they are so fickle that tomorrow — alas — they could well change their minds, thereby losing what today appears to them as the highest good in life. And so, while young people are in the happy state of being in love, they bind themselves. They turn that free, spontaneous love into a law, so that it can last forever. For someone who is spurred on by human love, this law is indissoluble marriage, contracted before God and people; for someone moved by the love of God it is a religious vow. In our case, the vow of poverty is a form of obligation, because once made, it binds you forever. But its "weight is sweet, its burden light," because it helps you to safeguard the choice your heart has made. At least, it should be so, and in fact is so for many.

That is why, having reached the end of this meditation, I am not going to spend much time suggesting practical ways of observing material poverty. There are in fact an infinite number of practical ways, which differ according to each person's state of life and profession. It would even be dangerous to draw up a set of rules valid for everyone. Practical rules and guidelines already exist, as I said: the ones each of us took on at our profession. Each person, through prayer and discernment with one's spiritual guide or superior, can easily discover what, in practice, the Spirit is asking of him or her.

For example, I know people who were asked by the Lord to give up, every so often, some object that was not strictly necessary, when they realized they had become a little too attached to it, as a way of keeping their decision alive and their heart free. Christ has also asked other people, whenever they were faced with a decision of some importance (buying something, going on a journey, choosing a type of car or clothes or furniture) to obtain not just the superior's permission if they lived in a community, but the Lord's permission in prayer. Sometimes the two can be different; the Lord can demand what a human superior today might not dare ask. Let us not be numbered among those who want to be poor, as long as they lack nothing.

When we talk about poverty today, in the context of a consumer society enjoying every material comfort, one biblical word automatically becomes essential — *sobriety*. It is one of the words that recurs most often in the New Testament, and is usually associated with vigilance. It indicates a capacity to moderate one's desires and to use things wisely without becoming enslaved. This is a biblical value which can be applied in extremely practical ways today.

We religious in particular need to be aware of the danger to our poverty that comes from having no children of our own. For parents, children are a constant reason to go without things, to give up something, to make savings — in a word, to be poor.

A father or mother will happily do without any number of things for the sake of their children, to give them the possibility of a better future than they themselves had! They think twice about spending any money on themselves when it's not strictly necessary. Not having this powerful natural incentive ourselves, and not even needing to worry about our old age since we have the support of a community, we run the risk of easily allowing ourselves things which most people would do without. The poor, the needy or the missions ought to be for us what children are for their parents: a ready incentive for our acts of self-denial and a constant reminder of the demands of our poverty.

I was saying earlier that the Spirit of Jesus living in the Church periodically sends out sparks that rekindle the ideal of poverty. Even today, here and there, we are seeing the rebirth of new offshoots of poverty. Sometimes these are religious communities, recently founded or renewed, where love for poverty and love for the poor go hand in hand, each feeding the other. Sometimes they are a new type of community, where consecrated and married people live side by side, having chosen a joyful and fraternal expression of poverty totally geared towards the proclamation of the Kingdom, and where every available resource is used for evangelization and spiritual animation. One evening when I was having supper in one of these communities, noticing the frugality of the meal and the joy on people's faces, I had a very clear impression of the atmosphere there must have been around St. Francis and his first companions. There are also ordinary Christian families who, having chosen Jesus as their Lord, decide to adopt a simple and poor lifestyle and refuse to sacrifice everything to their work or their careers. These small shoots, sprouting from a centuries-old trunk, herald a new springtime of poverty in the Church.

I will end with a word from Paul VI, part of his spiritual testament. "And what of the Church that was mine, to whom I owe everything? What shall I say to you? May God's blessings be upon you. Have a sense of the real, most profound needs of humanity, and be poor — meaning free, strong and loving — as you journey towards Christ."[27]

III

"You cannot serve God and wealth"

Spiritual Poverty:
an evil to be combated

In the account of Jesus' birth we see two starkly contrasting worlds: one symbolized by the inn, the other by the stable where He is born. The first world is all light, comfort and activity; people are eating, drinking, enjoying themselves. Rich people dressed in lavish clothes, with heavy purses on their belts, dismount from their horses and come and go at will. In the second world on the other hand, all is poverty, darkness, cold and discomfort. A young woman, silently accompanied by her husband, is about to give birth to her first child. They are forced to share bed and board with the animals.

Now let us look at the same scene through different eyes. Where was the greatest wealth at that moment? Where was the costliest treasure? In the inn or in the stable? And where are they now, all those people who found "room at the inn"? Who even remembers them? They are sunk in total oblivion, as though they had never existed. As for Mary and Joseph on the other hand, and the Child Jesus who was born in those circumstances, what significance do they have today for all humanity? What a reversal of fortunes!

We know of course that Jesus is always coming into the world anew. Christmas is more than just an anniversary, it is a mystery. Each year, something *happens*, it is not just *celebrated*. Even today, when He comes among us Christ finds, or rather creates, the same contrast. His presence alone reveals two different worlds. And we are called to take a stand, to decide which of the two worlds we wish to belong to, in reality as well as by right.

In these last two meditations we will be considering each of these worlds in turn: the world of the rich, the powerful, the satiated, and the world of the poor and humble — whose prototypes are Mary, Joseph and most of all Jesus. Our reason for doing so is to dissociate ourselves from the first world, to leave it behind and help others do the same, and to fall in love with the second, to enter it with renewed fervor and become part of it.

This meditation will deal with what we have called the bad sort of spiritual poverty: the poverty of the rich. The following one will deal with good spiritual poverty: the wealth of the poor. In the first case the expression "spiritual poverty" has an *objective* value, and means an actual lack of the goods of the spirit. In the second case the same expression has a *subjective* value and denotes the state of mind of someone who knows he has no resources of his own and so trusts totally in God. In the first case it denotes those who are poor "of" spirit, in the second, the poor "in" spirit, in their feelings, in their soul. If, as St. Francis used to say, good poverty consists in being "poor in temporal things and rich in virtue,"[1] then bad poverty consists in the opposite, being rich in temporal things and poor in virtue.

Because of its "negative" subject-matter this meditation will not be appealing or pleasant, but so much of the Gospel is at stake here that it would be impossible to pass over it in silence. If we did, we would be guilty of presenting a tame or watered-down version of the Gospel.

1. "You are poor!"

Keeping to our initial intention, we must let God's Word speak to us about the bad kind of spiritual poverty. For one thing, we would not want to lose ourselves in futile human arguments. There is in the New Testament at least one text where the word poor certainly does have the negative meaning we have stated. "You say: 'I am *rich*, I have prospered and I need nothing,'" says the Risen One to the representative of the Church in Laodicea, "but you do not realize that you are wretched, pitiable, *poor*, blind and naked" (Rv 3:17). Shortly before, the

Risen One had said the exact opposite to the Church in Smyrna: "I know your affliction and your *poverty*, even though you are *rich*" (Rv 2:9).

In the contrast between these two statements we find the whole Gospel teaching on riches and poverty summarized and applied to the Church. There is a type of human wealth which in the eyes of God is appalling poverty, and conversely, there is a type of human poverty which in God's eyes is enormous wealth. Indeed, "what does the rich man possess if he does not have God? And does a poor man lack anything, if he has God?"[2]

We can see in the Gospel some powerful moments in Christ's denunciation of what He calls "storing up treasures for themselves but not being rich in God's sight" (cf. Lk 12:21). But first we need to make a preliminary observation to clear the ground of possible misunderstandings: the Gospel never condemns earthly goods and riches in themselves. One of Jesus' friends is Joseph of Arimathea, "a rich man" (cf. Mt 27:57); Zacchaeus is declared "saved" even if he does keep half his goods for himself, and they must have been considerable. What Christ condemns is attachment to money and goods, trust in them as if "one's life depended on them" (cf. Lk 12:15). Such wealth is variously called "deceptive" (cf. Mt 13:22), "foolishness" (cf. Lk 12:20), an obstacle that brings the threat of "woe" (cf. Lk 6:24).

We should note that this evangelical denunciation of wealth has a double motivation: one appeals to *wisdom* and the other to *kerygmatic* or *eschatological* grounds. The first is based on the fact that it is folly to spend one's life amassing wealth when we know we could be summoned to leave this life at any moment, without knowing who would inherit our wealth: "You fool! This very night your life is being demanded of you. And the things you have prepared, whose will they be?" (Lk 12:20).

This motive is a traditional one inasmuch as it is already found in the Wisdom Books of the Old Testament. "(The rich man) says: 'I have found rest, and now I shall feast on my goods!'; he does not know how long it will be until he leaves them to others and dies" (Si 11:18 ff.; also Ps 49:17 ff.). "Do not be afraid when some become rich," says one psalm, "For when they die they will carry nothing away... Mortals cannot abide in their pomp; they are like the animals that perish" (Ps 49:17 ff.).

The eschatological motivation on the other hand is absolutely new, and once again has to do with the coming of the Kingdom. It is here that all the tragic danger of wealth is revealed. It makes it hard to enter the Kingdom, more difficult than for "a camel to pass through the eye of a needle" (cf. Lk 18:24).

We can judge just how serious is the nature of this "wealth which is poverty" by considering it from two different but complementary points of view: the *ontological* and the *historical*, in other words, in its relation to *being*, and to *time* or duration.

First of all, in relation to *being*, i.e., to the reality and intrinsic value of earthly goods. It was Pascal who formulated the famous principle of the three orders of greatness in which a person can reach fulfillment: the material or bodily order; the order of the intellect or genius; and the supernatural order of holiness and grace. There is a gulf separating each of these three orders from the other two, just as in nature there is a chasm separating the three kingdoms: animal, vegetable and mineral. Material riches neither add to nor subtract anything from genius, which moves on a different plane. Neither material nor intellectual greatness adds to or subtracts from the holy, which belongs to a different order of greatness that is witnessed by God and not by curious human eyes or minds. "Some," concludes Pascal, "are able to admire only bodily greatness, as though intellectual grandeur did not exist. Others admire only the intellectual, as if in the order of wisdom there did not exist some instances of greatness that are far superior."[3]

In the light of this classification, we might define someone who places all his boast in material wealth as "rich in a poor order"! The rich person deludes himself that he has reached the summit of the scale of greatness, unaware that above him are worlds of which he knows nothing. Rather like someone who had spent his life in the stables of a castle, not knowing what goes on in the upper floors, in fact unaware that they even exist.

Someone might ask on what do we base this scale of values, and the answer is simple. Material goods are by nature self-regarding and private. They never enrich anyone without at the same time making someone else poorer. Future generations are deprived of the goods we consume today without a second thought. They cannot be shared with others without in some way depriving those who possess them. In this sense Christ was right to use the word "unjust" about this type of wealth, which He calls "mammon" (cf. Lk 16:13). It always creates inequality, and is the source of endless jealousy, envy and division. It is therefore unjust, not merely because it is the fruit of injustice, but because it causes it.

Intellectual riches (art, philosophy, inventions) are at the half-way stage. They can enrich others if I wish them to do so, but they may not. In fact, they may even harm others if I use them wrongly for my own advantage (how many scientific discoveries have been used for war, or to manipulate life!). Spiritual resources on the other hand, by their very nature, are always transmissible and able to be shared. They never enrich one person without simultaneously enriching all. They unite rather than divide. If I enrich myself in faith, hope or charity, or grow in the grace of Christ (which are the things that Scripture calls true riches), not only do I deprive no one of anything, but, being absolute human values, they make all humanity grow.[4]

This explains why Christ in a certain sense

had to become poor in order to make us rich, and how it is that Paul can say: "Being poor, we make many rich" (2 Cor 6:10). It is by making oneself materially poor that others are enriched spiritually. It is a kind of law.

According to the other point of view, namely in relation to *time* or duration, we should not so much speak of being "rich in a poor order," as of being "rich in time and poor in eternity." In fact, "what can be seen is temporary, but what cannot be seen is eternal" (2 Cor 4:18): here, we are touching the core. Anything said about poverty stands or falls by one's idea of eternity. Without eternity it would be hard to escape the conclusion: "Let us eat and drink, for tomorrow we die" (Is 22:13; 1 Cor 15:32). This is why I believe no word more urgently needs to be brought back to life and put back into circulation than the word "eternity."

In the light of eternity the rich man resembles a poor beggar who one night has a beautiful dream. He dreams that he has suddenly inherited a huge fortune. In the dream, he is covered in splendid clothes and surrounded with gold and silver, the owner of fields and vineyards, so proud that he even despises his own father and pretends not to recognize him... But in the morning, he wakes up to find himself clutching a handful of flies.[5] So it is with the rich man who awakes in eternity. It was even less than a dream.

2. The idolatry of money, root of all evil

The word of God goes even further in its denunciation of unbridled attachment to riches. It calls such attachment idolatry: "Insatiable greed, which is idolatry" (Col 3:5; Eph 5:5). Mammon, or money, is not simply one idol among many—it is *the* idol par excellence. It is, literally, the "god cast in metal" (cf. Ex 34:17). We can understand why. Who is God's real enemy in this world, His competitor, objectively if not subjectively (in other words in reality, if not intentionally)? Is it Satan? But no man decides to serve Satan without a reason. He does it because he believes there will be some temporal advantage in it for him. Christ tells us clearly who the real alternative master, the anti-God, really is: "No one can serve two masters: a slave will either hate the one and love the other, or be devoted to the one and despise the other. You cannot serve God and wealth" (Mt 6:24).

Mammon is the anti-God because it sets up a sort of alternative world, it changes the object of the theological virtues. Faith, hope and charity are no longer placed in God, but in money. All values are perniciously inverted. Scripture says: "For God, nothing is impossible," and again: "Everything is possible to one who has faith." But the world says: "You can do anything if you have money." And on a certain level, all the evidence seems to agree. Karl Marx, author of one of the most penetrating analyses of money, speaks of "the alienating omnipotence of money." He writes: "Money, having the particular attribute of buying everything and appropriating every object, is therefore preeminently an object. The universality of this characteristic which it possesses constitutes its essential omnipotence... I am, in essence, that which is available to me through money, which I can pay for. My power is as great as the power of money. What I am and what I can do are not determined by my individuality at all. I may be ugly, but I can buy myself the most beautiful woman, therefore I am not ugly... Considered as an individual, I am a cripple, but money can buy me twenty-four legs."[6] (He is alluding to Mephistopheles' remark in Goethe's *Faust*: "If I can buy six stallions, don't their legs belong to me? I can ride them and feel perfectly at ease, as though I had twenty-four legs.")

But Marx's critique, though penetrating, is empty — it cannot change things. If the only human needs are economic ones, how can one prove that the power of money is in fact alienating and inhuman, since as he admits it serves wonderfully well to satisfy those needs? On that basis we shall not get much further than the traditional tirades and condemnations of money by poets and philosophers. Already, Virgil spoke of the "abhorrent greed for gold."[7] Shakespeare, too, had come up against it: "Gold? Thou common whore of mankind, that puts odds / among the rout of nations... thou visible god,

/ that sold'rest close impossibilities, / and mak'st them kiss!"[8] In a powerful synthesis, he calls money "the visible god."

Such cries of revolt as these are powerless. The god of money laughs at all of this. An effective critique of the alienating power of money is only possible if we know another order of wealth, a higher instance which stands in judgment over money and makes it relative. Christ did not confine Himself to describing or condemning the power of money: He crushed it. The Book of Daniel tells of an enormous statue with a gold head and feet of clay, symbolizing the kingdoms of the world. A stone, detaching itself from the mountain, struck the statue at its weakest point and smashed it to pieces. In the Christian interpretation of the story, the stone is Christ. His coming has smashed even the hardest empire to put down, which is the empire of Mammon.

Not only has He smashed it, He has given countless disciples of His the power to do the same. Money, which for the mass of people meant everything, to them meant nothing at all. Francis of Assisi's attitude of total refusal of money is well known, as a protest against the first onslaughts of that "alienating omnipotence" which were already apparent in his day, at the dawn of capitalism. "More than all other things he hated money" — so we read about him — "and advised the brothers to shun it as they would the devil incarnate, and to treat it like dung." He strictly forbade his brothers even to touch it.[9]

I once met an English businessman, a man of deep faith, who died recently. He wrote an article on the use of money and, at the end of it, there is a kind of personal testament which reads: "Money is a tainted thing, and the only way in which I will not be tainted by it is to use it honestly and generously. I must see it as a means to do good for others, and not as the foundation of my own happiness and security. I am only a steward called by God to use the talents and wealth that he has loaned me to build his Kingdom here on earth. I shall be judged for my stewardship and not for my wealth. I cannot use money to pay for a better lawyer, nor to bribe the judge. I can only use it to lay up treasure for myself in heaven by every little act of love and unselfishness towards the least of Jesus' brothers and sisters whom he sends to me for help."[10] Those who knew him know that this really was his rule of life. He too was one of those to whom Christ gave the power of conquering the god of money.

Scripture says "the love of money is the root of all kinds of evil" (1 Tm 6:10). When I was young I used to think this statement was a piece of hyperbole, to be taken relatively, not as an absolute. Now I am more and more inclined to take it literally. There are few sentences in Scripture that people today would be as happy to subscribe to as this one.

Behind every evil in our society there is money,

or at least there is *also* money. Money is like Moloch of biblical memory, to which young sons and daughters were offered up (cf. Jr 32:35), or the cruel Aztec god who had to have his daily quota of human hearts offered in sacrifice. What else lies behind the drug trafficking, which destroys so many lives, or the Mafia, the kidnappings, the political corruption, the arms trade? Recently, a doctor working as a volunteer in Rwanda, spoke on television. He showed the mangled bodies of people blown up by mines — mostly children playing, or mothers who had gone out in search of food or firewood. "To think," the doctor commented, "that for every one of these mangled bodies someone is making millions selling explosives and mines!"

Faced with a crime or a mystery, it used to be fashionable to say, *"Cherchez la femme,"* look for the woman! It would be much more accurate to say: *"Cherchez l'argent"* — look for the money! — because money is nearly always the instigator or motive. In the recent past, the almost mythical idea of an "Arch-Manipulator" gained ground in some countries: this was a cunning and extremely powerful character who was said to be working behind the scenes, pulling the strings and controlling everything for purposes known only to himself. It was a way of explaining the sudden political upheavals, the hidden power games, the terrorism and all kinds of mysteries afflicting society at the time. In fact, the "Arch-Manipulator" really exists, and his name is Money!

Like Christ, how often these days have we felt like crying out "You fool!" at the sight of people in responsible positions who hardly know which bank to use or where to hoard the proceeds of their corruption. Suddenly they find themselves in the dock or in a prison cell, just as they were about to say to themselves: "Now, my soul, enjoy yourself!" Who did they do it for? Was it worth the trouble? Did they really benefit their children or their families, or their party, if that's what they intended? Or did they instead ruin themselves and others?

In families too, the insatiable thirst for money and its excess nearly always destroys love, and then marriage. Many rich girls end up by not marrying, or systematically marrying the wrong person, because they suspect (with some justification): "Does he love me or my money?" Money, says Shakespeare in the play we quoted earlier, "this yellow slave / will knit and break religions, bless the accurs'd /… O thou sweet king-killer, and dear divorce / 'twixt natural son and sire! Thou bright defiler / of Hymen's purest bed! thou valiant Mars / thou ever-young, fresh, loved and delicate wooer."[11]

I once had an experience during a train journey. I remember it because it made me realize how widespread obsession with money is at all levels of society, not just in high society, and how much it alienates and dehumanizes people and impoverishes life. It was near Christmastime and this was a local line; everyone knew everyone else and spoke freely, so I couldn't help listening to their conversations. Along with all the positive, honest, hardworking features of their character, their talk also betrayed the one besetting sin of my own people. The sin grew like a deafening roar until I felt as if I were choking. And what was it called? Money! Money, money, money! All around me in that carriage, people talked about nothing but money from beginning to end: how much this tractor had cost, how much profit had been made on that deal, how much so-and-so had spent shopping, how much could be saved by doing this instead of that...

At one point I felt like crying out: "Brothers and sisters, is this really why Christ came into the world? Isn't there anything more to life than money?" But I didn't, and maybe I gave in to the sin of human respect. But that distress has stayed in my heart, perhaps waiting for an opportunity such as this, when I can shout these things not just to a few dozen people but (I hope) to thousands.

There is a lust for money that turns people into criminals and thieves, but we are not talking about that here. There is also a more discreet, apparently innocent thirst for money, which is actually taken for thrift and economy but in fact it, too, is idolatry. There is a popular meaning of the word "capital," very different from the sociological one, according to which capital is what you have managed to put aside, a source of pride and prestige among your neighbors, which is especially important when it comes to marrying a daughter or estimating the worth of a person or a family. "They've got good capital," people say admiringly; or else: "He's got no capital." But it also chokes all other sentiments, and causes quarrels and fierce rivalries, even among siblings, when it comes to decisions about how to divide property. Who could say this is a minor evil?

For people today, the parable of the guests invited to the wedding-feast could be repeated without changing a word. Someone gave a great dinner and invited many people. When the time came the first person invited said: "I have bought a piece of land, and I must go out and see it; please accept my regrets." Another said: "I have bought some oxen," and yet another said: "I have just got married" (cf. Lk 14:16). The list could be added to endlessly. Another said: "I've just mowed the hay and need to get it indoors before the rain comes"; another said: "I'm building a house and have to work on Sunday," and another: "I have to go to the football stadium to watch the game."

The story in the parable is already a sad one, but when you think of the reality it is much more tragic. The Father has sent His Son into the world; the Son died for us; He invites us to His table, saying: "Everything is ready, my love is ready for you, just come," but people don't care, and usually what holds them back is self-interest.

And what is the point of it all? St. Francis of Assisi, with a severity unusual in his writings, describes the fate of someone whose only purpose in life is to increase his "capital." Death is approaching, the priest is called and asks the dying man: "Do you want to be absolved from all your sins?" And the man answers yes. The priest continues: "Are you ready to make restitution for all the wrongs you did, and give back everything you cheated from your fellow men?" The man answers: "I can't." "Why not?" "Because I have left everything in the hands of my relatives and friends." And so he dies unrepentant, and as soon as he is dead his relations and friends say to themselves: "A curse on his soul! He could have made much more and left it all to us, but he did not!"[12]

The miser is the most miserable of men. Suspicious of everyone, he isolates himself. He has no feelings for anyone, not even his own family, whom he sees as using him, while they have only one wish as far as he is concerned: that he should die as quickly as possible so that they can inherit his wealth. Sparing no effort to scrimp and save, he denies himself everything in life, thus enjoying neither this world nor God, for it is certain that all his self-denial is not done for God. Instead of bringing him security and peace of mind, his money holds him hostage for ever. In the end, avarice is a real sickness, an obsession, but people are not usually born with it; it is something they fall into gradually through their own actions and choices. It's true that sometimes it is a reaction to a difficult or deprived childhood, but such cases are not hard to recognize and one can be more lenient in one's judgment.

If we move from what happens in the world and consider the Church, we can see how many evils have been caused over the centuries by attachment to money, even in the Church. What was behind the centuries of debilitating struggles between Church and Empire throughout the Middle Ages? Or behind the decline of dioceses, abbeys and monasteries at certain periods? "Wherever the corpse is, there the vultures will gather," Jesus said (cf. Mt 24:28). Wherever riches are concentrated, there the greed of the kings and lords of this world is targeted. The effect of the beneficiary and prebendary system was such that offices were not assigned on the basis of the sanctity and merits of individuals, but of rights and customs that had nothing at all to do with the life and interests of the Church. Ecclesiastical offices were reduced to ecclesiastical benefices, occupied by people who often never set foot in the diocese or abbey where they held titular office, and all they did was send their trustees out in due course to collect their revenues. Dante Alighieri represents this scourge of the medieval Church by the hungry wolf, the most ferocious of the wild beasts that bar the way to salvation — it is the beast "without peace," which "after its meal is hungrier than before."[13] In the struggle over Investitures, Pope Gregory VII had sustained an epic contest with the Empire to remove ecclesiastical offices from the secular power. The abuse soon resurfaced in another form during the rise of the nation States in Europe, and we know that the Protestant Reformation itself took the turn it did, especially in financial matters, because many bishops were conditioned by their rich possessions and had to obey other laws than those of Christ.

3. *"Apart from you I want nothing on earth"*

We now come to the most important part of this meditation: what use can we make today of this whole section of the Gospel, with its denunciations of the alienating and destructive power of Mammon?

The first thing to do is to *live* it, to let it challenge and judge us. We must first free ourselves of Mammon, so as to free others! We should thank God for the present state of the Church and the clergy on this point. We often complain about the bad times we live in, and the decline of faith. All this is true. But we easily idealize the past. We forget what the life of the Church was like for many centuries, when the Church even possessed a "State" — the Papal States — and bishops were also "princes." Church appointments have long since become once more what they truly are: ministries or services, not offices sought after for the worldly benefits they confer.

It is obvious, of course, that we have not yet

reached perfection, and never will. It may be good to remind the clergy of the need to avoid bombarding people with requests for money at parish, local and national level, because these often have the opposite effect, giving a false impression of the Church and alienating the sympathy of many. Experience teaches that where a good relationship exists between pastor and people, when the priest really gives his life for the flock, they not only provide for his needs but are happy to help and assist far beyond what is strictly necessary. It is so sad to hear that in some countries people leave the Church (hundreds of thousands of people every year) to avoid paying Church taxes, though I realize this is a complex matter which cannot be blamed on one single factor.

St. Peter reminds Christians that they were "not ransomed with silver and gold" (cf. 1 P 1:18), so money should be the last thing to keep people away from the fruits of redemption. We also have to avoid even the appearance of simony, that is, selling sacred things, setting too rigid a tariff for church services. People have begun to request openly that we have "the courage to review the entire system of church offerings, and separate them completely from liturgical celebrations." In some dioceses a start has been made in this direction.

St. Paul writes: "It is not your possessions I want, but yourselves. Children are not expected to save up for their parents, but parents for their children, and I am more than glad to spend what I have and to be spent, for the sake of your souls" (2 Cor 12:14 ff.). This suggests an important consideration for us: the money earned or saved by a prelate or minister of the Church in serving the Kingdom can have no fairer destination than the poor, because Christ Himself has made them His heirs and "exactors." Who should receive the royalties on everything that is written about the Gospel, if not the author of the Gospel, and hence the Church or the poor? The minister of the Gospel has a right to support himself from the Gospel, but not his nephews and relations!

But let us leave aside the negative aspects and dangers to be avoided, and concentrate on the positive ideal God's Word puts forward for believers, especially for clerics and churchmen, in this whole area. Rather than in the renunciation of riches, it consists in replacing them with a different kind of wealth. We know that St. Paul in his letters gives little space to condemning riches and money. He nearly always talks of riches in a positive way, because for him they mean the new kind, the true wealth which he calls the wealth of glory (cf. Rm 9:23; Eph 3:16), of grace (cf. Eph 1:7; 2:7; 1 Cor 1:5), and above all, of Christ. "The unfathomable treasure of Christ" (Eph 3:8) is what counts for him. Since they have Jesus Christ, the apostles are people who "have no possessions, yet possess everything" (cf. 1 Cor 7:30).

For a priest or Levite in the Old Testament the

ideal was to have God as his sole inheritance:

> "The Lord is my portion and my cup...
> The lot marked out for me is my delight:
> Welcome indeed the heritage that falls to
> me!" (Ps 16:5 ff.).

In the partitioning of the Promised Land, we know that priests and Levites were not assigned any portion of land, because the Lord was to be their heritage. And since the parcels of land were distributed by drawing lots, this is why the Levite says that the lot marked out for him is delightful. God is his delightful place. Today, God's words to Aaron are repeated by Christ to the priests of His Church: "I am your share and your possession among the people" (cf. Nb 18:20). The words "cleric" and "clergy" themselves derive from the word "inheritance," which in Greek is *cleros*. Sometimes we hear an Old Testament Levite, happy with this inheritance, joyfully exclaiming:

> "What else have I in heaven but you?
> Apart from you I want nothing on earth.
> My body and my heart faint for joy;
> God is my possession for ever"
> (Ps 73:25 ff.).

What a source of joy and security it is for a priest of the New Covenant to be able to make these words his own in times of temptation or doubt in his heart, applying them now specifically to Christ our Lord.

4. "Weep, you rich!"

The second thing we must do about the part of the Gospel we have been meditating on so far is to proclaim it. The false god of money must be attacked as decisively as the false god of sex. St. John Chrysostom makes a comparison between the two and concludes that love of money is worse than carnal love. In other words, that avarice is a graver vice than lust. "The lustful man," he says "loves bodies and the avaricious man loves riches, but the latter is worse because the power that draws him is smaller... On the subject of money, Christ says: 'If you do not give up all your possessions...' (Lk 14:33), but nowhere does he say: 'If you do not give up women.'"[14] No doubt that statement needs some qualification, but it is significant that such a rigorous moralist as Chrysostom felt moved to speak in such daring terms.

Our model in this proclamation about poverty and riches is Mary. In the *Magnificat* she declares: "He casts down the mighty from their thrones... and sends the rich away empty." She does not say "He *will* cast... He *will* send..." but "He casts... He sends" — she proclaims something that is as good as done. However, we might object: "Where, Mary, has this revolution you speak of happened? You know very well that the mighty, such as Herod, have remained firmly on their thrones, while the humble, such as yourself and Joseph, far from being raised up were obliged to seek refuge in a stable and flee to Egypt."

The fact is that Mary, on an impulse, has risen to the level of faith, where the change is actually under way, in fact it has already happened. She is witness to the fact — for the moment, the single solitary witness — that the Kingdom has come and has created a new scale of values. The old greatness, the old riches, now count for nothing at all, because a new greatness and a new wealth have appeared on the scene. It is like when there is a change of political regime in a country: the old currency is declared no longer legal tender and a new one is brought in.

Saint Irenaeus wrote that, on that occasion, "Mary cried out prophetically in the name of the Church."[15] She was the first to cry out what the Church is invited to repeat after her. We are coming to see more and more clearly that neither ideologies nor revolutions have succeeded in changing the situations of injustice and oppression of the poor which are a reality in so many countries of the world. Why don't we try Christ's method once more, which was to preach in the spirit of prophecy: "Woe to you who are rich, because you have received your consolation" (Lk 6:24)? I had never understood how terrible this word is and how much power it contains, until I once had to proclaim it in a place where the Mafia ruled undisturbed. There I understood that it was the only possible weapon.

On Christ's lips such a cry is far from being a cry of impotent rage. It is the pure and simple truth. Like all Christ's words it is a cry of love, a cry of sadness. And that is how it ought to sound on the lips of the Church. It would not then leave the rich so indifferent when they hear it. "Woe to you," indeed, because the calamity you are bringing upon yourselves is even greater than the misfortune you cause to others. You have already received your consolation, you have nothing more to expect in future: there is no future for you, except the fearful future judgment. How can you calmly go home at night and embrace your wives and children, knowing that in another part of the world there are fathers who, this very evening, will arrive home and not find their wives or their children, because they were killed by the mines which you made, or the drugs you put on the market?

Why do we not try to speak as the prophet Isaiah did against the big landowners of his day? "Woe to you, who join house to house and add field to field" (Is 5:8). Or use the language of St. James: "Come now, you rich people, weep and wail for the miseries that are coming to you. Your riches have rotted" (Jm 5:1). Here again, history does not record that in James' time corn suddenly began to rot in the granaries. But, like Mary, the Apostle is standing on a level that is much more real than the level of history. From now onwards, the really wealthy ones are the poor, whom God "has chosen to be heirs of the Kingdom" (Jm 2:5).

There are levels and aspects of reality that cannot be perceived with the naked eye, but only with infrared or ultraviolet light. Infrared pictures of entire regions of the planet can now be taken with the help of satellites. How different those regions appear! Another technique can even reveal what is hidden underground in a particular place, and this is how the sites of ancient cities and civilizations long buried were discovered. Well, thanks to the Word of God, the Church is able to give a different picture of life and of the world as it really is — the picture that God Himself has of them. We must never grow tired of putting this picture in front of people's eyes, again and again, before the image of this world, as we know it, has passed away and it is too late to discover the truth.

The situation of the Church in Laodicea is symbolic: "You say: 'I am rich, I have prospered and I need nothing'" (Rv 3:17). Today, behind that "you" lies an entire civilization glorying in its breathtaking technological achievements. It too is tempted to think of itself as rich, in need of nothing, not even of God. This is why the Risen Lord's reply is for our world too: "You do not realize that you are wretched, pitiable, poor, blind and naked" (*ibid.*). This is exactly the spiritual poverty of our so-called "First World"!

But we are not only called to denounce the idol of money and unjust wealth. Christ leaves nobody without hope, not even the rich. The disciples were dismayed at what Christ said about the camel and the eye of a needle. "Who can be saved, then?" they asked. He answered: "For men it is impossible, but not for God" (Mk 10:27). God can save the rich person too. We read in the parable of the rich man and Lazarus: "The poor man died and was carried to Abraham's bosom" — in other words, to a rich man's bosom, since Abraham was rich. We find a few poor shepherds around Christ's crib, but there are also kings with their gold. The point is not "can the rich be saved?" (that was never in doubt in the Christian tradition), but "what kind of rich person can be saved?" — and that is the title of a famous work by Clement of Alexandria.

Jesus points to a way for the rich to escape from their dangerous situation: "Store up for yourselves treasure in heaven, where neither moth nor rust consumes" (Mt 6:20), and again: "Make friends for yourselves by means of dishonest wealth, so that when it is gone, they may welcome you into the eternal homes" (Lk 16:9). Jesus advises the rich to transfer their capital abroad! But not to Switzerland — to heaven! "Many people," says St. Augustine, "are keen to bury their money in the earth, thus even depriving themselves of the pleasure of looking at it, sometimes for a lifetime, so long as they know it is safe. Why not bury it in heaven, where it would be far more secure, and where they could one day find it again, forever?" How are they to do this? It's simple, continues the Saint: "God offers you porters in the person of the poor. They go where you hope one day to arrive. In the poor person it is God who is in need, here and now, and He will repay you when you reach your destination. Not only that, but whereas in this world He forbids you to practice usury with your fellow men, He allows you to practice it with Him. God says: 'You have given me little; take much in return; you have given me earthly things; take eternal ones; you have given me what belongs to me; take myself as your reward.'"[16]

As we have already seen, almsgiving is not the only solution today. There are many other ways of using our goods to benefit the poor. One day a rich industrialist went to a cloistered nun for advice. He had decided to use his wealth in whatever way the Lord showed him, including selling everything and giving it to the poor, if that was what was asked of him. The nun asked for some time to pray and when the rich man came back for his answer she told him: "Have you got some money put by at this moment?" "Yes," he said. "Well, go and open another factory and give jobs to some more workers!" And that's what he did.

The Bible sketches a kind of portrait of the rich Christian, which lists the things he must and must not do in order to be saved. The Apostle Timothy writes: "As for those who are rich in the present age, command them not to be haughty, or to set their hopes on the uncertainty of riches, but rather on God, who richly provides us with everything for our enjoyment. They are to do good, to be rich in good works, generous, and ready to share, thus storing up for themselves the treasure of a good foundation for the future, so that they may take hold of the life that really is life" (1 Tm 6:17-19).

Every year a crib is set up in St. Peter's Square. Standing there right at the center of the colonnade it is a fine symbol of the Church welcoming the Child Jesus, enfolding Him in an embrace of faith and love. What a contrast there is between the hut at the foot of the obelisk and the Basilica of St. Peter behind it! However, the one does not necessarily contradict the other. Christ did not prevent the "very costly" perfumed oil being poured on His head, in fact He defended the person who did it. He did not, as the Pharisees wanted to, prevent the people from laying palm branches for His entry into Jerusalem.

And yet, how much we need the reminder that the crib gives. It should almost be left there all the year round. But if that is not possible, at least we should leave it standing in our hearts. In a certain sense, the Basilica with all its lights and splendor ought to remind us of the heavenly Jerusalem we are bound for, the glory of the resurrection which Christ has entered. The hut stands for the Church in this world. The former is our destination, while the latter is our way. We cannot reach the one without passing by way of the other. There is no entry into Jerusalem except by way of Bethlehem.

Like the shepherds after they had heard the angel's message, we too should make the firm resolution: "Let us go to Bethlehem!"

IV

"Blessed are the poor in spirit, for theirs is the Kingdom of Heaven"

SPIRITUAL POVERTY: AN IDEAL TO STRIVE FOR

What the soul is to the body, the fruit to the tree and the flavor to the fruit, such is spiritual poverty (having "a poor person's soul") in relation to the material kind. A body without a soul is dead; a tree without fruit is sterile; and fruit without flavor is insipid. So also is material poverty unless accompanied by spiritual poverty. However, just as the soul cannot live and act without a body, and fruit cannot blossom unless on a tree, and flavor cannot emanate except from a fruit, the same is true of spiritual poverty compared to material poverty.

The two things, then, cannot be separated, even though we are dealing with them separately. Still less can the one be opposed to the other, since each requires the other. Christianity has never advocated a disembodied spiritual poverty that could dispense with real poverty altogether, or even coexist with material excess. Anyone who tried to do so would soon be disowned by the Church's healthy sense of what is right. It is true that today something of the kind is talked about, called the "Prosperity Gospel," but this is clearly an aberration and is hardly worth considering.

On the other hand, never has the Gospel or the Church canonized material poverty in itself, or measured the heroism of poverty by the extent to which it lacked material things. There is however an infinite variety of ways in which material and spiritual poverty have blended together, in varying degrees, in the life of each saint in each succeeding age. This is understandable in view of the doctrine about charisms, and the various functions exercised by each person in the body of the Church.

So, it is now time for us to say something about "the soul of every form of poverty," about its fruit and flavor, which is spiritual poverty. Let us at once listen to God's Word, which will light up our way like a beacon. In Matthew's Gospel this word is heralded by an unusually solemn introduction: "Seeing the crowds, Jesus went up the mountain, and after He had sat down, His disciples came to Him. Then He began to speak, and taught them, saying…" (Mt 5:1 ff.). We are attending a kind of liturgy, the original Liturgy of the Word.

The crucial thing each time is to manage to make that leap of faith which turns us into "contemporaries" of Christ. We become those disciples, that place becomes this place, that day becomes today, so that Christ's word does not reach us as reported speech or a simple quotation, like bottled water, but directly, like water gushing forth right now from the Spring who is the Risen Lord, alive in the Spirit. The word which gushed forth from our Savior's lips on that day, and today flows out for us too, is:

> "Blessed are the poor in spirit,
> for theirs is the Kingdom of Heaven"
> (Mt 5:3).

Jesus compares His word to a seed, and this seed has grown into a giant tree, blossoming in every season of the Church's life, "filling the earth" and "bearing much fruit."

By what audacity, and for what purpose, are we now proposing to enlarge on this word (which in the Gospel hardly takes up one line) and write several pages of commentary on it, when an infinite number of pages has already been written? The justification is that Scripture is a living organism, and every word is a vital part of a larger whole, and receives fullness of meaning from that totality. Each word must be made to resonate within the whole of the Bible and Tradition, as in a kind of echo chamber, so that it acquires its proper full-bodied sound. As soon as we hear the single note, we need to be able to hear, in our mind's ear, the "chord" of which it is a part.

Ideally, every biblical text is situated at the point where two overlapping circles touch, as in the center of a figure 8. Starting with the text itself, two research processes should begin, one encompassing all that precedes and leads up to the text in the Bible; the other, all that the text itself has set in motion in the rest of the Bible and in the life of the Church. This is what we would now like to do, starting with the second of these two processes. Obviously, it will not claim to be a complete study, but simply provides the stimulus to apply the Word to our own times, so that it finally moves us to action, with all the weight and authority of the Bible and Tradition that lie behind it.

1. The "poor" and the "poor in spirit"

Regarding the beatitude of the poor there is, first of all, a literary problem connected with the way it is presented in the Gospels which we must at least mention. The problem is that the beatitude is referred to rather differently by Matthew and Luke. One addresses the poor indirectly: "Blessed are the poor," the other directly: "Blessed are *you* poor"; one says poor "in spirit," the other simply "poor." Which version is closer to the original thrust of Christ's preaching?

Nearly all exegetes hold that the expression "in spirit" was added by Matthew. The discovery of the expression "the poor in spirit" (*aniye haruah*)[1] in the Qumran texts has shown that it was part of the Jewish language and spirituality of the time, but that alone is not enough to show that the phrase comes from Jesus Himself, since Matthew the evangelist reflects a similar background and could therefore have introduced such a phrase into the text himself.

The most plausible explanation seems to be that Matthew and Luke both depend on a common source which simply says "poor." Luke, being concerned to stress the social implications of the term as well, keeps it as it is and in fact reinforces it by contrasting it to "you... rich" (Lk 6:24). Since Matthew's intention is catechetical, he is concerned to expound the religious meaning that the word "poor" had in Jewish spirituality and in the thought of Jesus, so he adds "in spirit." In doing this he is merely applying a very standard principle in the redaction of the traditional material. The same concern to bring out the moral implications of Jesus' words is also found in the succeeding beatitudes. For example, "the hungry" becomes, in Matthew, "those who hunger and thirst for justice."

In recent years, especially during the Council, these differences have become the object of heated debate. Some, favoring Luke's reading, stress the social significance of the beatitudes, and see in the word "poor" a social condition first of all, an actual state. (This is the interpretation adopted by the various liberation theologies.) Others base themselves more on Matthew and stress the religious significance. "Poor in spirit" would indicate an interior attitude rather than a social status.

The latter exclude the idea that Christ wanted to beatify an entire social class. Only a spiritual situation — they argue — can be related to a spiritual reality such as the Kingdom. That real poverty is a privileged road to spiritual poverty is very true and Jesus says so again and again in a thousand different ways; nevertheless one must not think that the beatitude is targeting the proletarians or the so-called "people of the land" in the Judaism of the day. The true poor person in the Gospel is God's devotee, the one who has staked everything on God, by faith. In the Judaism of the time, the term "poor" was practically synonymous with holy (*hasid*) and pious, or godly.[2]

Others have reacted against this interpretation by saying that it places too much emphasis on the inner dispositions of the poor person, and too little on the nature of the coming Kingdom. The beatitudes, they claim, are first of all a revelation about the mercy and justice that must characterize God's Kingdom; they are a revelation about God, rather than about humanity or the poor. The word for poor used in the Gospel (*ptochos*) indicates the destitute, the unfortunate, those who need alms in order to survive. The corresponding Hebrew term, *anawim*, originally indicated people who were "bent over," in other words abased, humiliated and oppressed. They are obliged to bend before those who are stronger and richer than themselves.

For what reason, it could be asked, should such people be favored by God? The answer is, not because of any particular religious "merits" or good dispositions of their own, but because God owes it to Himself, as a just king, to defend the defenceless. According to Old Testament mentality the poor are those "protected by the king": it was not a matter of retributive justice, which rewarded the merits acquired by the unfortunate, but of a munificent, regal justice. In faithfulness to Himself, God is obliged to guarantee the rights of those who are not in a position to assert them by their own methods.

But how in that case does one explain the persistence of the state of poverty and oppression of the poor, even in Israel? That the theory is disproved by the facts does not lead to the conviction of God's regal justice being abandoned. Instead, it is projected into the future, to God's Kingdom of the end times. Then the poor will be avenged against all their former oppressors, then they truly will enjoy the benefits of God's care and concern. The God who "casts the mighty from their thrones and raises those who count for nothing," and who "fills the starving with good things and sends the rich away empty-handed," will appear as the perfect fulfillment of the ideal king. The religious significance of the beatitudes remains, but it is a theological, not an anthropological significance. It is based on God, not on human beings.[3]

Cardinal Lercaro, who played a key role in introducing the theme of poverty into the Council's discussions, said on that occasion that the poor had to be understood "in the usual sense of that term." Jesus did not intend to recognize "the merits of a few of His hearers and to promise them a reward," but that His was a "teaching about the totally gratuitous mercy of God," in which "moral dispositions" are of no importance whatever. The only thing that counts is that Christ was sent to console them.[4]

These, then, are the two main interpretations of the beatitude of the poor. One relies more on poverty as a "state of mind," the other more on poverty as a "social status." In both cases deliverance from poverty comes from the Kingdom, but in the first case it presupposes a disposition in people, while in the second, it is a demand that God makes of Himself. Taken in isolation, neither of these two positions satisfies completely: the first, because it tends to exclude too completely any reference to social factors and the reality of poverty; the second, because it excludes too drastically the inner dispositions of the poor person.

I would particularly like to stress the drawbacks of the second interpretation, which seem to me more serious. It does not explain the close relationship that exists in the Gospel between the concepts of poverty and humility, between the privilege of the poor and that of children. In any case, it is an interpretation that boils down to nothing at all. According to this interpretation, the Kingdom of God constitutes the great deliverance of the poor, sociologically speaking. But when one then goes on to analyze the nature of that Kingdom, one can see that it brings nothing new to their real situation, because on the material level it makes them neither richer nor more replete. So this modern interpretation is only apparently more attentive to the social aspect. In fact, there is a danger of exploiting poverty, turning it simply into an occasion for God to demonstrate His sovereign justice. Even in that case the fulfillment of the promise would be situated on an altogether different plane from the promise and the expectation: the poor person is promised deliverance from material poverty, but in the end the deliverance turns out to be only of a spiritual nature.

Certainly Jesus is concerned for the real poor, but not so much when He proclaims the poor "blessed." Rather, He shows this concern when He says that whatever is done or not done to them, He considers as done to Himself, and when He threatens with hell those who have no concern for the poor, as in the parable of the rich man and Lazarus.

In our case the difficulty arises from the use of the category of "merits" and "virtues," when we ought to use the category of faith. God is not induced to act in favor of the poor by their merits or moral dispositions, but because they are more ready to believe. What God appreciates in the poor is not so much what they have, but rather what they do not have: the pride of the self-sufficient who are closed in on themselves, expecting salvation by their own efforts alone. To think otherwise would be like saying that the tax-collectors and prostitutes are offered the Kingdom first because God prefers such a "state," rather than because sinners are capable of repentance and the false just are not.

The question is not whether God's action presupposes something in advance (it obviously does not: "Who has ever given a gift to Him, to receive a gift in return?"), but whether it requires something *in response*. The poor person has to recognize and welcome this preferential offer on God's part: in other words, he has to believe. As St. James says: "Has not God chosen the poor in the world to be rich in faith?" (Jm 2:5). The Gospel beatitude, "Blessed are the poor in spirit, for the Kingdom of heaven is theirs," should be read in the light of the grace-faith polarity: "By grace you have been saved through faith" (Eph 2:8). Here, the "Kingdom" represents the offer of grace, and "in spirit" represents the response of faith. The poor "in spirit" are the poor who are "believers." It is as if Jesus had said: Blessed are you poor, "because you have believed" (we must not forget that He is talking to actual people who had followed Him, just as in the "woe to you" passages He is talking to people who had in fact rejected Him). Or, Blessed are you "if you believe," or "because you are readier to believe." Faith is the background to every word Jesus speaks.

The solution to the difficulties therefore has to be sought in a synthesis of the two positions. Luke's "poor" and Matthew's "poor in spirit" must be united, not contrasted. By adding the expression "in spirit," Matthew was not only acting in the interests of catechesis, but also of hermeneutics: he was bringing out an element that was implicit, but real, in the concept of poverty as Jesus used it.

From all this we can see how wise the Council was to accept and insert into the Constitution on the Church the call to poverty, and equally, how wise it was not to accept the particular interpretation of poverty that was current at a time of strong social tensions, which would have impoverished the concept of poverty itself.

In this way the great principle of Tradition is confirmed: not replacement, but development. The traditional interpretation of poverty is not overturned, but enriched. The Fathers of the Church had interpreted poverty in spirit almost as synonymous with humility, or else in the sense of the monastic practice of "voluntary" poverty. St. Basil (to quote only the leading authorities) answers the question "Who are the poor in spirit?" by saying: "Those who have become poor because of the Gospel teaching, or those who accept as God's will the poverty in which they find themselves for whatever reason."[5] St. Augustine replies: "The humble man is poor in spirit."[6]

Putting the two elements (humility and choice) together, Chrysostom replies: "The poor in spirit are the humble and contrite of heart... There are many who are involuntarily poor, by necessity: the Lord is not speaking to them." For him, the true poor are "the humble and contrite in spirit," spoken of, for example, in Isaiah 66:2.[7]

This traditional interpretation, which was brought to perfection in the way of spiritual childhood of St. Teresa of the Child Jesus, has been *enriched*, thanks to recent discussions, by greater attention to the sociological and existential dimensions of the poor, but it has not been *replaced* or repudiated.

2. The biblical ideal of poverty in spirit

Having taken a look at what *came after* the text — its "achievements" and interpretations in the Church — we can now return to the actual text and try to see what preceded it and prepared the ground for it in the Bible itself. I do not intend to trace the entire history of how the ideal of "the poor of Yahweh" came to be formed in Israel. Instead I will try to highlight the essential features of that ideal which, if we live them today, can make us, too, truly poor in spirit.

There are two features, one negative and the other positive, which are best summarized in this oracle of the prophet Zephaniah, who was one of the first to formulate the ideal:

> "For I will leave in the midst of you a people
> humble and lowly.
> They shall seek refuge in the name of the
> Lord —
> the remnant of Israel" (Zp 3:12 ff.).

The *negative* element, expressed here in terms of humility and poverty, consists in the absence of self-sufficiency and pride, whether individual or national, and in the recognition of personal sin and the need for salvation. This is a new, religiously more refined, way for a human being to stand before God. In fact it represents a real qualitative leap in the development of humanity's religious sense. The outlines of that "sense of dependency" are beginning to appear: that quality proper to the creature in the face of its Creator, which some have claimed constitutes the very essence of religious sensitivity. In this, humanity no longer perceives itself only as God's ally or subject, who can claim certain rights and credit before God by observing the law and fulfilling the requirements of worship. Rather, it sees itself as totally dependent on God for everything, and can only relate to God as a debtor, in a spirit of pure gratitude.

Even the sense of national pride, inherited from the golden age of the monarchy, gives way to a sense of poverty and smallness. We read in Daniel:

"For we, O Lord, have become fewer than any other nation, and are brought low this day in all the world because of our sins" (Dn 3:37). It is in this context that the idea of the contrite heart and the humble spirit, so close to poverty in spirit, is born (cf. Is 66:2; Dn 3:39).

The *positive* aspect or element that goes hand in hand with this sentiment is unconditional trust in God, or "trusting abandonment": "The remnant of Israel shall seek refuge in the Lord." The so-called "psalms of the poor" are full of moving expressions of trust in God: "This poor man called, and the Lord heard him" (Ps 34:7); "As for me, I am poor and needy, but the Lord takes thought for me" (Ps 40:18). These psalms start from a concept of poverty with social connotations (weak persons exposed to exploitation by the rich and powerful) and eventually reach an exquisitely religious meaning, where "poor" is the equivalent of "just" and "upright" (Ps 140:13 ff.) or "humble" and "small."

Humility and trust in God, the two essential elements of this ideal of spiritual poverty, are marvelously joined in what is known as the psalm of spiritual childhood:

> "O Lord, my heart is not proud…
> As a child has rest in its mother's arms,
> even so my soul.
> O Israel, hope in the Lord
> both now and for ever" (Ps 131:1, 2-3)

The messianic ideal, too, shows traces of this new spiritual awareness. The Messiah himself comes to be seen as the first ancestor of this poor and humble remnant: "Look, your king comes to you, triumphant and victorious, humble and riding on a donkey" (Zc 9:9).

Jesus embraced this spiritual ideal and brought it to perfection. As always, He first of all lived it and then proclaimed it in His Gospel, giving it its definitive expression in the beatitude of the poor in spirit. He tells us to learn from Him, for He is "meek and humble of heart" (Mt 11:29), an expression which, bearing in mind the biblical meaning of the terms humble and meek, could easily be translated as "poor in spirit." He is born of a poor young girl in a milieu totally permeated with the ideal of the "poor of Yahweh." He surrounds Himself with people who have no claims to greatness. He fulfills even in a material way the prophecy of the humble Messiah riding on a donkey (cf. Mt 21:4 ff.).

Later on in His preaching he instils the two ideals of humility and trust. On the one hand, humility, contrition, rejection of any attempt to save oneself by one's own merits, as in the parable of the Pharisee and the Publican; on the other, absolute trust in the heavenly Father, who feeds even the birds of the air and the lilies of the field (cf. Mt 6:24-34). He often brings the two characteristics together in a favorite image, that of becoming a child, so much so that the Gospel "could be read as the Gospel of the child."[8]

So it is that, starting with Mary's *Magnificat*, we find two contrasting categories of people depicted in the Gospels: on the one hand, the rich-powerful-satiated-wise; on the other, the poor-humble-hungry-small. One day Jesus "exulted in the Holy Spirit" over this fact, and exclaimed: "I thank you Father, Lord of heaven and earth, because you have hidden these things from the wise and the intelligent, and have revealed them to infants" (Lk 10:21). St. Augustine comments: "He does not say, 'You have revealed them to the ignorant and the stupid,' but 'You have revealed them to infants.' Who are the infants? They are the humble. O the way of the Lord! Either it did not yet exist, or it was hidden so that it could be revealed to us!"[9]

3. How to live the beatitude of the poor

Now the moment has come for us to stand before this word of Jesus: "Blessed are the poor in spirit" with a slightly different attitude from the one we have cultivated until now: no longer the attitude of someone trying to *understand*, but of someone determined to *act*. "If you know these things, you are blessed if you do them" (Jn 13:17): the blessed are not those who *know* everything about the poor in spirit, but those who *are* poor in spirit.

Let us first apply poverty in spirit to the Church. As we saw, the ideal of spiritual poverty was applied to an entire people before it came to be applied to individuals: "I will leave in the midst of you a humble and lowly people." This messianic people is represented today by the Church. Therefore we are talking about something that has to be a feature of the Church as a whole, as an institution and as the People of God.

The change that took place in Israel, when it passed from simple trust in its own political and religious resources (the Law, the monarchy, worship, the Temple) and from a vague feeling of superiority over other nations, to an altogether new sense of poverty, minority and religious diaspora, was a real conversion in the true sense. Trust in self was replaced by trust in God alone, with no attempt to use God and immediately translate that trust into human certainties and guarantees, as some did in time of danger when they put their minds at rest by repeating: "This is the temple of the Lord, the temple of the Lord" (Jr 7:4). It was at this time that the prophets called on Israel to stop wanting to play a role among the great powers of the day, and to turn to God alone as its sole support.

Does all this mean nothing to us? If the political and diplomatic aspect of the Church's life cannot be abandoned altogether, it ought at least to be more and more imbued with this spirit of poverty we have been discussing, with its "nuncios" aware of being "messengers," certainly, but "apostolic" in the sense of being sent by a poor and humble king who rides on a donkey, a king born in a stable who died on a cross.

This spiritual difference and otherness cannot be demonstrated without the Church agreeing to be different, even in externals, from the corresponding political institutions of the world: in structure, bureaucracy, titles, customs, language, style, in everything. Vatican embassies in the countries where they operate are "foreign" in a much more radical sense than other embassies. They represent not only another *State* but another *world*. During a retreat I was asked to give some years ago to the Ecclesiastical Academy (the institution responsible for training future Apostolic Nuncios), I showed them a picture of Our Lord in Pilate's Praetorium: crowned with thorns, with a clown's cloak on his back and his hands bound with a rough rope. Then I said to them: "Take a good look at this Jesus and make sure His image is etched in your minds, because one day, if you go forward on this way, He is the one whose messengers and representatives you will be."

This process, thanks be to God, is now under way, especially since the Council years — particularly on the level of the witness of individuals' personal lives. For someone like me, looking at the Church of today from a background of study of much earlier ages, the change appears almost miraculous. During the retreat I just mentioned, I remember observing the President of the Academy at prayer, and I'd say to myself, "You've a long way to go before you resemble this servant of the Church!"

However, God's Word urges us not to stop at the beginning or only halfway. Sometimes, changing external structures is more difficult than changing hearts. Father Gauthier, in one of his "messages to the Council" wrote these words: "The hope of the poor is, first and above all, to meet Jesus Christ the carpenter who lives in His Church, to be able to recognize Him when they meet the Church. The poor and the workers want nothing to do with a Church that calls itself the bride of Christ and gives itself the airs of a grand lady... How can a spouse dress and live differently from the way her husband wants her to be and loves her?"[10]

Christ's poverty was first of all a rejection of all prestige. The search for prestige is not necessarily a bad thing, but we need to be clear about what we mean by prestige. The word is ambiguous; in fact it is one of the world's greatest idols. Christ taught His followers to put prestige in exactly the opposite place to where the world places it. "Anyone who wishes to be first among you must be the slave of all," He said (Mk 10:44). Evangelical prestige does not consist in excelling in honor and prestige, but excelling in humility and service. The true ecclesiastical "career," the one that counts in the eyes of Christ, is certainly a promotion, but promotion downwards. To speak of the "prestige of the Church" without this qualification is a contradiction in terms.

Such spiritual poverty is necessary at all levels of the Church's life, not only at the top. St. Peter recommended presbyters not to "lord it over" people in their charge (cf. 1 P 5:3), and St. Paul protests that he too does not wish to "lord it over" the community (cf. 2 Cor 1:24). One way of behaving like lords instead of servants or models for the flock is to administer the community's property (the church, buildings, various structures and funds), and to grant or refuse their use, as if they were my exclusive property, rather than as goods held in common about which the whole community, through its representative bodies, has the right to have its say. In this connection it is instructive to note how the Apostle administers the funds obtained in the collection. He asks for delegates chosen by the churches — not by himself — to be with him, so that no one can have any grounds to criticize him for the large sums he administers (cf. 2 Cor 8:19 ff.; 1 Cor 16:3). In the Apostolic Exhortation *Pastores Dabo Vobis*, published after the Synod of Bishops on priestly training, we read: "Being personally involved in the life of the community and being responsible for it, the priest should also offer the witness of a total 'honesty' in the administration of the goods of the community, which he will never treat as if they were his own property, but rather something for which he will be held accountable by God and his brothers and sisters, especially the poor."[11]

The ideal of spiritual poverty, as we have said, always includes great trust in God, as the positive side of not trusting in oneself. Sometimes, perhaps without realizing it, we speak as if the future of the Church were uncertain, or at the mercy of historical events, popular movements and social changes. Asked what Christians should think about the prospect of Christianity apparently set to become a religious minority in the world, Pope John Paul II answered by quoting Jesus in the Gospel: "Do not be afraid, little flock," and reminding his questioner that "the Gospel does not promise easy successes, though it is at the same time a great promise."[12] This is true.

The future of the Church is in the hands of the Risen Christ, to whom "all power in heaven and earth" has been entrusted, so it is in good hands. We have had endless confirmation of this fact in twenty centuries. That is why Christ tells us: "Do not worry. Today's troubles are enough for today" (Mt 6:34). Each age, too, has its own share of troubles.

Our friend Péguy, the poet, puts these words into the mouth of God:

> "They tell me there are men who cannot
>   sleep,
> proficient in their work, but not in rest.
> How can they have so little trust in me?

During the day they manage their affairs,
but will not let me manage them at night.
As if I can't be trusted for one night.
They will not let my wisdom govern their
affairs.
Oh you wise men! You might well find
you could entrust your plans into my hands,
and find them, in the morning, unimpaired
or only slightly spoiled!
Perhaps I could still run things for a
while."[13]

Anxiety and worry about tomorrow is "the trap which only free beings can fall into." To cure us of these things, Jesus would have us learn from the birds of the air and the lilies in the field. However, more is expected from human beings than from birds or flowers. They have no concept of danger or of tomorrow, precisely because they are not free and conscious beings. But "perfection means to know the danger, to see it with your own eyes, to be fully awake, to be able to experience worry about material things, but nevertheless to overcome fear by faith and trust, so that we are truly free of anxious thoughts, with the carefree confidence of faith."[14]

There is a beautiful present we can give to the Child Jesus, and that is to lay down all our concerns, all the anxieties that keep us awake, all the useless worries, before His crib, as the shepherds laid their baskets in front of Him. We should remember what Christ said to His Apostles in the boat, after He had calmed the storm: "Why are you so afraid? Do you still have no faith?" (Mk 4:40).

4. Poverty and the return to unity

The Fathers of the Church were guided in their reading of the Bible by a principle which they summed up in the words: "*Ecclesia vel anima*," both the Church and the soul. In other words: everything written in the Word of God is always to be applied on two levels: one concerns the Church, the other the individual believer. So I would now like to try to show what the principle of spiritual poverty might mean for a believer today as we approach a new century and a new millennium.

We have already said that the justification for poverty is to be found in sin, which drives human beings to "separate themselves from God and turn to creatures." But perhaps this is not the ultimate reason in an absolute sense. Even without sin, there would still be a reason to give up the indiscriminate possession and enjoyment of things, even good things. God has set human beings in the midst of the variety of creation, not so that they might settle down once and for all in that situation, thinking it definitive and setting up their "three tents." He has done so, not so that they would remain static and satisfied in the midst of so many good things, but would set out on a journey from multiplicity to unity, towards the sole and supreme Good, and that this would be an achievement in which they too had cooperated through detachment, choice, and the actual exercise of freedom.

By giving humanity the commandment to "love God with all your strength" as the first commandment, God was inviting men and women to concentrate on one single love, thereby in a certain sense inviting them to renunciation and poverty. "To love God," says St. John of the Cross, "means divesting oneself of everything that is not Him."[15] We are made for unity, made "to be, in some way, the totality." If it were a question of a material totality, one would try to reach the goal by increasing, adding to, expanding, constantly acquiring new things and new pleasures. But since a spiritual totality is involved, we must take the opposite route and proceed by way of decrease, subtraction and surrender, attaining the whole by starting from the opposite end, by reversing the route, one might say. It is as if someone standing on the African shore of the Straits of Gibraltar tried to reach the European shore by circling the entire Mediterranean, while someone else dived naked into the sea and swam across the Straits, reaching the same destination after a few strokes. This is the way of poverty. Thanks to it, the movement of "creation leaving God," has given way to the movement of "creation returning to God," which is the achievement of the redemption.

This explanation of poverty found its most celebrated expression in the mystical school called the Rhine School. Meister Eckhart has a famous sermon on the beatitude of poverty in which he states that a man is poor in spirit when he "wants nothing, knows nothing and has nothing." With regard to *not wanting*, poverty means that a person should be "as divested of his own created will, as he was when he did not yet exist." As for *not knowing*, poverty is "not knowing anything about anything, neither about God, nor creatures, nor oneself"; not even claiming to know whether or how God acts in oneself, renouncing every activity that belongs to memory, intelligence and imagination — which by its nature is dispersive — and standing still at the point where all things are one, and where ignorance and knowledge coincide. As to *not having*, poverty in spirit means no longer having even a place of one's own in which God can act, but that "the person should be so free of God and of all His works that God, if He wants to act, must Himself be the place in which He wills to act."[16]

The Rhine mystics were not the only ones who said things like this. Poverty in spirit is also presented in this way by St. John of the Cross, though he avoids certain excesses found in the former. He calls spiritual poverty "nakedness," which he defines as the renunciation of those goods which can remain in the soul, such as desires, appetites and consolations. The truly poor person is one who has "placed all things into that nothingness."[17]

In order to understand these statements, we must put them into the context of the overall vision which their authors had. There are *two dimensions* in human beings: one is "essential," like a single and stable nucleus, and is called the "depths of the soul," which relate with God directly; the other is "accidental" and multiple, and expresses itself in the different faculties (the will, the intelligence, the memory) and in the senses, which extend the soul's activity outwards. The first level is that of *being*; the second, that of *doing*.

Consequently, in human beings there are also *two movements*: one is a movement within, towards the depths of the soul, involving the cessation of all activity and willing, in which spiritual poverty therefore takes effect. The other is a movement outwards and towards action (willing, knowing, having). The first movement, called "irruption" or "invasion," is a return to unity; the second, called "eruption" or "e-vasion," is a movement towards multiplicity. God is to be found at the conclusion of the first movement. Hence the importance of poverty in spirit, which is not only an ascetical virtue but a mystical one.

However, what happens at the conclusion of this journey back to interiority? A Nativity takes place, "the Birth of God in the soul." In a Christmas sermon, Meister Eckhart himself expounds upon this mystical event in all its splendor and audacity.[18]

"What good is it," he repeats with Origen, Augustine and many others before him, "that Christ was born once of Mary in Bethlehem, if He is not born again in me?" The depths of the soul are the very place, the crib or manger, where this birth comes about. "It is necessary, therefore, that the soul in which this birth is to take place should keep itself absolutely pure and alive with a perfect nobility, should be one with and in itself, not dissipating itself in the multiplicity of creation through the five senses, but inwardly in union with itself in that which is its purest possession." In this case too, the Word comes down from heaven "while all is wrapped in profound silence" (cf. Ws 18:14). No one can enter into those "depths of the soul," not even the soul itself, but only God. Here, as He does in eternity, God pronounces His "eternal Word," and it is born.

And in what *manner* does all this take place? Precisely through spiritual poverty. A person cannot provide a more favorable environment in which God can act in this way than by detaching himself not only from things but also from all his or her activities and ideas. "If you divest yourself of yourself and of everything external, then you will truly receive Him in His fullness." Therefore "withdraw from the flurry of external actions! Flee from the tumult of outward activities and inner thoughts, which only produce restlessness."

And what is the subsequent fruit of all this? Not only does the Father beget His Son within you, but you yourself are begotten as a child of God and receive power. "The light shone in the darkness: it came to what was its own (the depths of the soul!), and all those who welcomed it received the power to become children of God" (cf. Jn 1:5, 11-12).

We may wonder whether an ideal which is apparently so remote from reality still has any usefulness for us? These authors never tire of repeating that such experiences are not reserved to a very few, but are accessible to all the baptized, indeed, in a certain degree, to all mankind. And we today are perhaps in a position to recognize the truth of their conviction. At least we can understand how this doctrine, worked out by a whole generation of exceptional people concentrated in the Rhine valley during the fourteenth century, can have a providential impact in our own times. The teaching certainly needs to be purified of some exaggerations and dangers, which in any case the Church had already begun to do while the authors were still alive. But this should not surprise us. If "our prophesying is imperfect" (1 Cor 13:9), so too is our mysticism.

Understood in its inspirational core and its essential elements, this vision can offer the Church of today the means by which to respond to one of its most serious challenges, which comes from the fascination exerted by other religious traditions. And it can do so while remaining consistent with its own spiritual heritage, announcing to the people of our day the very things they go looking for elsewhere, "gropingly, as in the dark."

There is no doubt that the characteristic movement of our present civilization is not that which Eckhart calls "irruption," but "eruption," not the return to unity but the thrust towards multiplicity; not the tendency towards being, but towards doing and having. We know how harshly traditional spirituality — for example that of *The Imitation of Christ* — has been criticized for being totally geared towards interiority and flight from the world. It has been countered by a spirituality of social and political commitment, a so-called "religion of the second commandment," which goes out to the world and wants to transform it.

Unfortunately, however, we had not realized that this movement was grafting itself onto another, moving in the same direction and duplicating it. The fact is that the whole of our culture is also geared to action, to the transformation and conquest of the world. We are living in the age of mass communications. Communication, the need to be informed about everything in the shortest possible time, is the daily obsession. But by acting in this way, human beings are becoming further alienated from their own center, and from the very source of their energy. This leads to the fragmentation of the human person, and the mystics we have looked at explain why this happens. "Every faculty that flows outwards is imperfect... If your eye wants to see all things, and your ear wants to hear them, and your heart wants to have them all present, then your soul will inevitably be fragmented and dispersed into all these things."[19] This explains the "weakness" of which we are beginning to become aware. Ours is not only the age of "weak thinking" as has been said, but there is also a weakness of the will, of the memory, and of the arts. Mythology often speaks of a divinity smashed into pieces, whose fragments have been dispersed throughout the universe. The same is happening to the human soul. There is a diaspora of the soul, which causes the soul to be scattered and dispersed to the four winds.

But what is happening in the meantime? Something in humanity is rebelling against this profound alienation, and there are signs of it in various fields. The most interesting sign for us, and the most disturbing, can be seen precisely in the field of religion. More and more people, even Christians, are turning to other religions, especially of Buddhist inspiration, which seem to promise humanity a way back to unity from dispersal and multiplicity, by way of direct contact with that reality or consciousness (or as the case may be, the absence of reality and consciousness) which is variously called God, or All, or Nothingness.

Now we know that the treasury of the Church contains quite another response to this emerging need in modern man, and it is here that we see the positive side of interfaith dialogue. It challenges each person to be better aware not only of the specific features and differences of one's own faith, but also of the as yet unexplored potential of one's spiritual heritage. It challenges us to give our own answers to other people's questions — answers that come from within.

5. "Go back inside yourself!"

Does the ideal built up on the basis of the evangelical beatitude of spiritual poverty offer anything new? The answer seems clear, especially if we complement Meister Eckhart with Augustine, who is often his source. "Do not go outside," Augustine exhorts us; "Go back inside yourself, for truth dwells in the inner man."[20]

"Go back inside yourself!": many people agree on this point. But Christianity adds: "Truth lives in the inner man," or rather "Christ lives in the inner man."[21] We are talking about a Person, not an abstract "Truth." Having reached the center of himself, in the starkness of his own being, man finds not only himself, or silence, or the absence of everything, or emptiness. He finds instead the Being, the Word, the Presence, the Fullness. In your inmost heart, the Father "gives you His eternal Word and in that very Word He gives you His own life and essence and godhead, absolutely."[22]

Does this mean that everything ends in the

negation of action, of practical charity, of the need to go out to the world? On the contrary: this renewed contact with the center and source of one's own being — and therefore with God — "will enlighten both the soul's faculties and the outer man. The reason is that no sooner does God touch the depths with His truth, than light is cast over the faculties also, and in that instant the person acquires more knowledge than anything he had ever been taught."[23]

This is also confirmed by everyday experience. All the great enterprises or actions that have had a real impact on the course of the spiritual history of humanity have always emerged from a long period of silence. Therefore the message from Eckhart and the mystics in general is not that one should abandon one's commitments and retire once more from the world, but that one should "reestablish the balance and the vital rhythm between exteriority and interiority, between unity and multiplicity. We need to rediscover the riches contained in the depths of the soul, so as to pour them into human relationships, which can only be saved through the inner renewal of individuals."[24]

The world today urgently needs to rediscover this balance. We are threatened with spiritual asphyxia, especially in the modern megacities where all is deafening and blinding exteriority. People have strayed so far from home that they can no longer find their way back. We ministers of the Word and "servants of the Spirit," as the Apostle defines us (2 Cor 3:8), must humbly place ourselves at their service in this matter, so that our young people will not have to go to the Far East in search of someone who can help them find themselves and, in the process, discover God.

How are we to prepare ourselves for the task? Above all by being the first to return to the heart of things, truly celebrating that "Nativity of the soul" which has been put before us. As we were saying in relation to material poverty, the first thing to do is to fall in love with this ideal, and ask the Holy Spirit to "attract" us, to draw us towards it. And then to begin practicing it, at least in small things.

What we have heard from the Rhine mystics about spiritual poverty is sublime indeed, but perhaps still too abstract and speculative to be translated into practice. So here is the humble Francis of Assisi showing us a few concrete steps we can all begin to take: "There are many people," he writes, "who spend all their time at their prayers and other religious exercises and mortify themselves by long fasts and so on. But if anyone says as much as a word that implies a reflection on their self-esteem or takes something from them, they are immediately up in arms and annoyed. These people are not really poor in spirit. A person is really poor in spirit when he hates himself and loves those who strike him in the face." For Francis, a person is poor in spirit when he "takes no more pride in the good that God says and does through him, than in that which He says and does through someone else."[25] There is a long way to go, at least for me!

Life offers us many opportunities to exercise spiritual poverty in this way. A disciple of the Poor Man of Assisi, Blessed Angela of Foligno, says that true poverty of spirit is such that the soul "can perform works without any intention and without concern for any merit."[26] It is thus that the beatitude of the poor in spirit leads to that of the pure in heart. Let us therefore begin, or continue, our struggle against "ulterior motives." "O, love of poverty, kingdom of peacefulness," exclaimed another great mystic,[27] indicating that poverty was also the way to another beatitude, that of the peacemakers.

Before we conclude, let us turn our thoughts to the historical and liturgical Christmas. What does it represent, after all we have heard about the mystical Christmas which the soul experiences? Does it pale by comparison? On the contrary, the historical event of Christmas makes all mystical repetitions of it possible and validates them. Christ can be born in me because He was once born of Mary in Bethlehem. The reality of Christmas is also the sign and the model of that invisible Nativity. It was in extreme poverty, in silence, in the most profound tranquillity and peace, that the almighty Word first descended from its royal throne, and light shone in the darkness. This is a reminder to us of the conditions necessary for the Nativity to be reenacted in our souls.

A text of Vatican II says that Mary "stands out among the poor and humble of the Lord, who confidently hope for and receive salvation from Him."[28] In other words, she is the perfect fulfillment of the ideal of spiritual poverty that we have tried to reconstruct. She walks at the head of that remnant of "poor and humble ones who trust in the Lord." She had no need to "go back to the heart" of things, because she never strayed from it. Her gaze, her every thought, especially while she was carrying Jesus in her womb, was entirely directed within, since within her truly dwelt, "in reality and not only spiritually, He who is 'the Truth'."

During the whole time I was preparing these reflections I had before my eyes an icon of the Madonna with the Child Jesus in her arms wearing royal vestments. Her face, turned towards her Son in an attitude of boundless humility and adoration, expresses the quintessence of evangelical poverty. If there is even one single thought of any value in these reflections of mine on poverty, I am convinced that it came from her. That icon has been my textbook on poverty.

May she obtain for us the grace to love poverty, and to be numbered with her among those "poor and humble ones who trust in the Lord alone."

Footnotes

Introduction

[1] *Approved Rule* of 1223, chap. 2 (St. Francis of Assisi, *Omnibus of Sources*, Franciscan Herald Press, Chicago, 1973, p. 59).

[2] Cf. Y. Congar, *Vraie et fausse réforme dans l'Eglise*, Cerf, Paris, 1968, II, chap. 1.

[3] St. Isaac of Nineveh, *Ascetic Discourses*, 4, Città Nuova, Rome, 1984, p. 89.

[4] St. Gregory the Great, *On Ezechiel* I, 11, 5 (PL 76, 907 f.).

[5] Cf. S. Kierkegaard, *For Self-examination*, Oxford University Press, 1946, p. 64.

[6] Cf. J.F. Kavanaugh, *Faces of Poverty, Faces of Christ*, Orbis Books, Maryknoll, New York, 1991.

Chapter I

[1] J.-P. Sartre, *La Nausée*, in *Oeuvres romanesques*, Gallimard, Paris, p. 105 f.

[2] Pope Paul VI, *Evangelica testificatio*, 17 f. (*Enchiridion Vaticanum* 4, p. 649 f.).

[3] St. John Chrysostom, *Homily on Matthew* 50, 34 (PG 58, 508 f.).

[4] Cf. *Life of B. Pascal*, written by his Sister Gilberte.

[5] Sulpicius Severus, *Vita Martini* 3 (ed. J.W. Smit, Milano, 1975, p. 13 f.).

[6] St. Leo the Great, *Discourse 2 on the Ascension*, 2 (PL 54, 398).

[7] J. Guitton, quoted by R. Gil, *Presencia de los pobres en el concilio*, in "Proyección" 48, 1966, p. 30.

[8] R. Hobbs, *The Desire of my Heart*, ed. Elisa Hobbs, London, 1995, p. 49.

[9] In "Acta Apostolicae Sedis," 54, 1962, p. 682.

[10] J.M. Tillard, *Pauvreté Chretienne*, in "Dictionnaire de spiritualité," 12, col. 667.

[11] Card. J.B. Montini, *Christmas and poverty* (Address given on 25 December 1959).

[12] Pope Paul VI, *Evangelica testificatio*, 18 (*Enchiridion Vaticanum* 4, p. 651).

[13] "Dominus conservet eum et vivificet eum et beatum faciat eum in terra et non tradat eum in animam inimicorum eius."

Chapter II

[1] Cf. J. Dupont, *Les béatitudes*, vol. 2, Gabalda, Paris, 1969, Section II, chap. 2.

[2] *"Per foramen acus." Il cristianesimo antico di fronte alla pericope evangelica del giovane ricco* (Studia Patristica Mediolanensia, 14), Milano, 1986.

[3] Clement of Alexandria, *Quis dives salvetur*, 16, 3 (GCS 17, p. 170).

[4] *Lumen gentium*, 8.

[5] In "L'Osservatore Romano," 1 December 1994, p. 4.

[6] St. Augustine, *On the Gospel of John*, 32, 8 (CCL 36, p. 304).

[7] St. Thomas Aquinas, *Summa Theologiae*, IIIae, q. 106, a. 2.

[8] *Ibidem*, q. 106, a. 1.

[9] In "Acta Apostolicae Sedis," 73, 1981, p. 521.

[10] St. Augustine, *On the Gospel of John*, 26, 45 (CCL, 36, p. 261 f.).

[11] Cf. J. Alvarez Gomez, in *La povertà religiosa*, Istituto Claretiano, Roma, 1975, p. 79.

[12] In "L'Osservatore Romano," 1 December 1994, p. 4.

[13] Celano, *Second Life* 162 (St. Francis of Assisi, *Omnibus of Sources*, Franciscan Herald Press, Chicago, 1973, p. 534).

[14] Dante, *Paradiso*, XI, 84.

[15] St. Thomas Aquinas, *S. Th.* III, q. 40, a. 4.

[16] Blessed Angela of Foligno, *Complete Works*, Paulist Press, New York, 1993, p. 304.

[17] St. Gregory of Nyssa, *On the Beatitudes*, 1 (PG 44, 1201).

[18] St. Augustine, *De Genesi ad litteram* 11, 15, 20 (CSEL 28, p. 348).

[19] St. Augustine, *Confessions*, VIII, 1, 2.

[20] St. Bernard, *Sentences*, III, 94 (*Opera omnia*, 6, 2, Rome 1972, p. 152).

[21] A. Hornung, in *La Povertà religiosa*, cit., p. 52.

[22] Dante, *Paradiso*, XI, 71 ff.

[23] St. Augustine, *Sermo* 14, 9 (PL 38, 115 f.).

[24] St. Bernard, *Discourses* 2 (*Opera omnia*, 5, Rome, 1968, p. 364 ff.).

[25] *Imitation of Christ*, III, 37 ("nudus nudum Jesum sequi").

[26] Cf. J.M. Tillard, *Pauvreté chretienne*, in "Dictionnaire de spiritualité," 12, coll. 664 ff.

[27] Pope Paul VI, *Thoughts on death*, Libreria Editrice Vaticana, 1979.

Chapter III

[1] St. Francis of Assisi, *Approved Rule*, cit., chap. 6.

[2] St. Augustine, *Sermo* 85, 3.3 (PL 38, 521).

[3] B. Pascal, *Pensées*, n. 793 (ed. Brunschwicg).

[4] Cf. S. Kierkegaard, *Christian Discourses & the Lilies of the Field*, trans. Lowrie, 1939.

[5] Cf. St. Augustine, *Sermo* 39, 5 (PL 38, 242).

[6] K. Marx, *Economic and Philosophical Manuscripts* of 1848.

[7] Virgil, *Aeneid*, III, 57 ("auri sacra fames").

[8] W. Shakespeare, *Timon of Athens*, act IV, sc. 3.

[9] Celano, *Second Life* 35, 65 (*Omnibus of Sources*, cit., p. 98).

[10] R. Hobbs, *Money: A Tainted Thing?*, in "The Month" 2, 1989, p. 77.

[11] Cf. W. Shakespeare, *Timon of Athens*, cit.

[12] Cf. St. Francis of Assisi, *Letter to All the Faithful*, 12 (*Omnibus of Sources*, cit., p. 98).

[13] Dante, *Inferno*, I, 49 f.

[14] St. John Chrysostom, *Homilies on the Letter to Titus*, 5,2 (PG 62, 689).

[15] St. Irenaeus, *Against the Heresies*, III, 10, 2.

[16] St. Augustine, *Sermo* 38, 8f. (PL 38, 239ff.).

Chapter IV

[1] QS IV, 3.

[2] Cf. A. Gelin, *Les pauvres de Jahvé*, Paris, 1953; cf. also by the same author: *Les pauvres que Dieu aime*, Paris, 1968.

[3] Cf. J. Dupont, *Les Béatitudes*, 2 vols., Paris, 1969.

[4] Cit. by J. Dupont in *La Chiesa del Vaticano II*, Vallecchi, Florence, 1965, p. 410, n. 76.

[5] Cf. St. Basil, *Shorter Rules*, 205 (PG 31, 1217).

[6] St. Augustine, *Sermo* 53, 1 (PL 38, 365).

[7] St. John Chrysostom, *Homilies on Matthew*, 15, 1 (PG 58, 224).

[8] Pope John Paul II, *Letter to the Children*, in "L'Osservatore Romano," 16 December 1994.

[9] St. Augustine, *Sermo* 67, 5, 8 (PL 38, 436).

[10] P. Gauthier, *Jésus, l'Eglise et les pauvres*, in "ICI," 15 December 1962, p. 26.

[11] Pope John Paul II, *Pastores dabo vobis*, 30 (AAS 84, 1992, p. 705f.).

[12] Cf. John Paul II, *Crossing the Threshold of Hope*, chap. 17.

[13] Cf. Péguy, *Le porche du mystère de la deuxième vertu*, in *Oeuvres poétiques complètes*, Gallimard, Paris, 1975, p. 657 f.

[14] S. Kierkegaard, *Christian Discourses & the Lilies of the Field*, (=Edifying Discourses, 2), trans. Lowrie, 1939.

[15] St. John of the Cross, *Ascent of Mount Carmel*, II, 5, 7.

[16] Meister Eckhart, *Sermon* 52 (ed. J. Quint, München, 1952).

[17] St. John of the Cross, *Ascent of Mount Carmel*, I, 3, 4; III 13,1; Letters 16.

[18] Meister Eckhart, *The Eternal Birth* (translated into Italian by G. Faggin, *Il Natale dell'anima*, La Locusta, Vicenza, 1984, pp. 17-33).

[19] *Ibidem*, p. 42 f.

[20] St. Augustine, *De vera religione*, 39, 72 (CCL, 32, p. 234).

[21] St. Augustine, *On the Gospel of John*, 18, 10 (CCL, 36, p. 186).

[22] Meister Eckhart, *Sermon* 49 (ed. J. Quint, München, 1952).

[23] Meister Eckhart, *The Eternal Birth* (ed. cit., p. 12 f.).

[24] G. Faggin, *Il Natale dell'anima*, cit., p. 12 f.

[25] St. Francis of Assisi, *Admonitions* 14 and 17 (*Omnibus of Sources*, cit., pp. 83 and 84).

[26] Blessed Angela of Foligno, *Complete Works*, Paulist Press, New York, 1993, p. 196.

[27] St. Catherine of Genova, *Life*, chap. 39 (ed. Cassiano da Langasco, Genova, 1987, p. 59).

[28] *Lumen gentium*, 55.